Galactic News
FROM THREE ANGELS

PRESENTED BY
LONNIE MELASHENKO

WRITTEN BY
DAVID B. SMITH

VOICE OF PROPHECY

Published by:
Voice of Prophecy
101 W. Cochran Street
Simi Valley, CA 93065

Cover design by Zero Crossing Graphics

ISBN 0-9703940-1-2

Printed in the United States of America

CONTENTS

1

DIDN'T THE WORLD END IN 1994?

You're about to embark on a wonderful . . . scary . . . hope-filled
. . . challenging . . . Scripture-based . . . and mysterious adventure.
It's a journey that goes right into the heart of one of the Bible's
most challenging books – Revelation. But not only that, we're
going to leap, by faith, right into the very middle of the book, one
of the most intriguing passages in the Word of God.

Now I have to tell you something right up front. Ironically – and
it's been pointed out to me on many occasions – this book comes
to you from a radio ministry known as The Voice of *Prophecy*. For
more than seven decades, the concept of Bible prophecy, the study
and preaching of Bible prophecy, has been right in our name. It's
been a hallmark of our organization: not just in our over-the-air
broadcasting, but in our Bible study lessons, in the meetings that
we've held around the world. I remember how when I was just a
boy myself, attending a Christian "academy" in Singapore, Pastor
H. M. S. Richards, Senior, and the King's Heralds would circle the
globe with their great prophecy meetings. Those were thrilling
adventures, and here in a new millennium, those key Bible truths
about end-time events are more timely than ever.

Any person who decides to study this marvelous book, though,
should proceed with boldness, but with very *cautious* boldness.
Here's why. The book of Revelation is filled with Christian truth,
and with Christ as the focus . . . but it's also replete with mystery.
Names and numbers and beasts and images. And you know, it's so
possible to put things together in a way that seems right to YOU
and start constructing your charts and time lines. A hundred years
ago our spiritual ancestors probably used a banner in a big tent;
today our brightest evangelists are probably highlighting the same
concepts with Microsoft PowerPoint slides or CD-ROM visuals.
And a Christian writer or a preacher on the radio has to be very

careful not to hit you with a bunch of verses and say: "A leads to
B, B leads to C, and here are the dates and here's what it all
means, and we're right, and that's the end of it. Start packing your
Samsonite suitcases for the great tribulation."

In other words, we have to be humble. Very humble. SUPER-
humble. Especially in a media ministry where people are joining
us from all spiritual walks, from all churches and from no church
at all.

I have right here on my desk in front of me, this very minute, a
book written by a Christian in my own church. Here's the title of
it: *WARNING! Revelation Is About to Be Fulfilled*. Well, that's a
good title. I believe that to be a true statement. But this particular
writer, and this was a layman's publication, not an officially
"blessed" or endorsed book, looks at the themes of Revelation –
the beasts and the metaphors and the empires of history – and then
says, right at the end: "A big year is coming." (This was published
in 1991, by the way.) "Yes, a significant year is coming. The
great global earthquake of Revelation 8 is coming, and I think
something very momentous is coming up . . . in the year . . .
1994."

Well, guess what? 1994 came and went rather quietly, and we're a
good ways down the road from there. Unless you count the
Northridge quake as a global, Armageddon-type event, I don't have
to spell out the moral to the story, do I? Any time we study
Revelation, a big dose of Holy Spirit-sent humility and brother-
hood and hand-in-hand team study . . . that's the only attitude we
can take.

Will you join me in that? This entire book is devoted to just studying seven verses. Not from the easy part, if there is any such thing
in Revelation. But from the very core of the book – chapter 14.
People in my own Adventist church family love to explore these
particular verses and ponder what they mean, and maybe you've

been through them as well. And now, step by step, in this brief journey together, let's see together what Jesus might have for us here in what we call "The Three Angels' Messages."

In Chapter Two I'm going to suggest to you the very bold idea that YOU . . . might well be an angel. What do you think about that? But for right now, let's just read the very first verse of this intriguing Bible puzzle. Here's Revelation 14:6: "And I saw another angel fly in the midst of heaven, having the everlasting gospel to preach unto them that dwell on the earth, and to every nation, and kindred, and tongue, and people."

Just that one verse is so rich in wonderful meaning that we could explore it for years. But let's make some observations right here. First of all, this is an end-time message. This is a message for the last days in human history. Earlier in Revelation, and in the somewhat parallel prophecy book of Daniel, the Bible takes us on a prophetic journey outlining four great world empires: Babylon, Medo-Persia, Greece, and Rome. And then extending down beyond the rule of Rome, beyond the tumult of the Middle Ages, and into the final generations of earth's history, these proclamations in Revelation come into view.

And here in verse six, an angel flying in the midst of heaven is proclaiming "the everlasting gospel." In a very exhaustive Bible commentary series published in my own denomination – which admittedly does love to study this passage – the writers make this crucial observation: "There is but one gospel to save men. It will continue as long as there are men [and women] to be saved. There never will be another gospel."

My friend Pastor Henry Feyerabend, who preaches on television up in Canada, says this in his book, *Revelation Verse By Verse:* "The everlasting gospel never changes. There is only one gospel, first announced in Eden and to the children of Israel, and it is proclaimed anew in every generation. It meets the needs of every crisis in the world's history."

So here in these "Three Angels' Messages" is the news about the everlasting, always true, never-changing gospel. Which is this: JESUS SAVES. Listen, that's the gospel! And right here in all the mystery, two truths come cutting through the prophecy fog without any distortion, any confusion, any possibility of misinterpretation. First of all, this message is for the whole world: "every nation, and kindred, and tongue, and people." Which means, without a doubt, that YOU are included. This message is shouting out, as you skim these pages, to YOU. And the two words God's messenger is sending you, at full Revelation volume, are so simple: JESUS SAVES.

That's what this first glorious angel has to say. Right now. To you.

Have I got your attention? Good. Keep on reading!

TWO ANGELS NAMED DAVID AND LONNIE

Okay. It's time for me to defend that proposition that YOU . . .
might actually be an angel. Now, I don't have any way of knowing yet what kind of e-mail volume that suggestion might bring in
to Box 53055, Los Angeles. But I stand by that amazing statement: you – yes, I mean YOU – are an angel.

Now, before you begin pinching your own arms and legs to see, or
looking for your birth certificate, let me share a marvelous story
about angels . . . and then let's go right to the Word of God, which
is always our protection when radio preachers come up with, shall
we say, "colorful" things.

A few years ago, an ambitious young Christian woman determined
that she was going to make it in Hollywood – for the purpose of
getting enough clout that someday she would be able to tell God-
oriented stories, on television, her own way. So she paid her dues;
she delivered coffee; she did the producer's laundry; she drove
scripts around town and counted paper clips. And bit by bit, she
got to the point where, yes, she could pretty much get a TV program made.

This story, by the way, is from the recent bestseller, *How Now
Shall We Live?*, by Charles Colson and Nancy Pearcey. The young
lady's name: Martha Williamson. Which, if you've been watching
CBS in recent years, you recognize; she's the top producer, and
often the scriptwriter, for the Sunday night megahit: *Touched By an
Angel*.

But here's the inside story. CBS had actually set her up to do the
very thing she had always dreamed about: a program about angels.
Angel's Attic, it was called. The only problem was: the program
was terrible. The script was bad. It featured unbiblical concepts:

the angels argued with God, and didn't want to do what He told them to do. They fought and bickered among themselves. It was kind of a "cop show with wings." So . . . Martha said no. On principle, she wouldn't do it. She had another writing offer from another network, and was going to pursue that.

But somehow a still small voice told her to go back to CBS. Take a second look. Unfortunately, the job that was formerly hers for the asking – now she'd have to interview for it. She might not get it, plus she could lose the new offer from the rival network. Martha's agent, needless to say, was not pleased.

Well, she went into the meeting and faced the big brass at CBS. They still wanted her; that was the good news. But the show was still a turkey, and she began to tell them straight out *why* it was a turkey.

"First of all," she told them, "angels don't disagree with God. They don't argue with God. They're His messengers; they love to obey Him; they instantly obey Him."

"But . . . but . . . that's not very dramatic," they protested. "We need conflict and snappy dialogue, not obedience."

"Can't do it," she said.

"How come?"

And she leveled them with this. "Because the Bible SAYS this is the way it is. This is truth. Angels obey."

Incredibly, the big shots at CBS blinked, and said okay. Issue number two, Martha said, was that the program suggested that when people died and went to heaven, they became angels. "What's wrong with that?" the "suits" wanted to know.

And she gave them the same answer. "It's wrong because the Bible says so. Angels were created by God back at the beginning of time; people on earth don't turn into angels. They just don't. The Bible says so; case closed."

Oh. And there was a long pause. Finally, after dotting some I's and crossing some T's, CBS let her do *Touched By an Angel* her way. And the rest, as we say, is history. Millions of viewers around the world tune in every week to watch these three obedient angels – Monica, Tess, and Andrew – tell people how much God loves them, and that He has a plan for their lives.

Well, what does this have to do with Revelation chapter 14? And what does it do with the rather bold statement I just made – flatly contradicted by Martha Williamson, by the way – that you might be an angel?

Several things, actually. First of all, you and I are not angels. I admit that. My wife comes close; I admit that as well. But we are all human beings on this sorry old earth; God made us as sons and daughters of Adam, and He created His holy angels up in heaven, and never the twain shall switch sides. When you die, you don't turn into an angel; that simply is not taught on a single page of Martha Williamson's Bible or yours either.

Having said that, let's turn again to the first verse in this thrilling but mysterious prophetic Bible passage right in the heart of Revelation: "And I saw another angel" – the first of three – "fly in the midst of heaven, having the everlasting gospel to preach unto them that dwell on the earth, and to every nation, and kindred, and tongue, and people."

Again, we find that two great pillars of eternal truth come piercing through the mystery of Revelation's beasts and metaphors. First of all, this is the everlasting gospel the angel is proclaiming. The "eternal" gospel, says the New International Version. It's for every people group, every language group, every tribal group, every demographic group on the face of Planet Earth. And it's for these last days, which means you and me right here in the 21st century. This angel is talking to us.

But right here is the point that really makes me excited. Because I don't believe that God is really going to send one solitary angel, or even three of them, to fly through the sky and preach this eternal gospel to a lost and dying world. That's not what's being taught here. This great job, this commission, isn't going to be given to three angels, whether they're named Tess, Monica, and Andrew, or Gabriel, or any other cherubic name. I believe that people just like us – preachers, non-preachers, old people, young people, missionaries, and backyard-barbecue witnessers – are the people who are going to tell the world this everlasting gospel.

In the *Seventh-day Adventist Bible Commentary* for Revelation 14, the writers make this very point: "The angel represents God's saints engaged in the task of proclaiming the everlasting gospel.... It is, of course, true that literal angels assist men [and women] in the task of proclaiming the gospel, but this is not the predominant idea here."

So here are three angels pictured in Revelation. And they have an everlasting gospel message, a never-changing, always-true, eternally-the-same message to share. It's two words long: JESUS SAVES! But despite the metaphor of an angel, or three of them, doing this job, it's not really them who do it. It's US! And I can prove it!

Two verses, both of them in the Gospel of Matthew, nail this down. The first one, spoken by Jesus, is in chapter 24, verse 14. The great promise for the end time: "And this gospel of the kingdom will be preached in the whole world as a testimony [or witness] to all nations, and then the end will come."

That's a great promise, but it doesn't say who should do the job. Jesus was talking to His disciples, but He doesn't spell out that it's their assignment. But go over just four chapters to the final words of Matthew, chapter 28, verses 18-20, and this is too clear to be missed. Jesus again, to His followers: "All authority in heaven and on earth has been given to Me. Therefore go and make disciples of all nations, baptizing them in the name of the Father and of the Son and of the Holy Spirit, and teaching them to obey everything I have commanded you. And surely I am with you always, to the very end of the age."

"Even unto the end of the world" says the King James. And there you have it. Fact: if you're a Christian – in fact, if you've only been a Christian for the last 24 hours or 24 minutes – then you are an angel. Your little voice is part of this great first angel's message in Revelation 14. And so is mine.

I'd like to think that The Voice of Prophecy radio ministry, 70-plus years strong now, is part of that first angel – telling a listening world, "Jesus saves." You know, especially at Christmastime, there's one week of our programs that literally is uplinked via satellite and the network of Adventist World Radio . . . and it truly does hit the entire planet. That is unbelievable! And it's part of that Revelation angel's message.

Have you noticed lately, sometimes, that when you log onto the Internet and maybe use something like CompuServe or AOL, the home page will have a Christian theme right up front? You can click on a banner, and here is dialogue about some spiritual issue, a verse-of-the-day, a place to register your feelings on a certain belief in the faith. People writing about Jesus Christ and His claim on our lives. I've seen that a number of times, and just get hit by goosebumps. Because that message, "Jesus saves," hitting the whole planet over the Information Superhighway, is a fulfillment of Revelation 14 that Pastor H. M. S. Richards, Senior, could never have envisioned.

So this angel, flying in the midst of heaven, is actually – when you get right down to it – YOU. And me. But what does it all mean?

3

RUNNING FROM THE COPS

Maybe you noticed a controversial news story back not too long ago coming out of our United States Supreme Court. The official docket description was kind of sterile: "Illinois vs. Wardlow, 98-1036," but the essence of the case was actually very colorful. Nine black-robed judges said that police have the right to chase, and stop, and question, and search a person for the simple reason that they had run away from those same police. Even if you haven't committed a crime, if they cruise by, and the sight of that black-and-white cop car makes you break into a quick jog in the other direction, they can then go after you, pat you down, and see what you've got on you. This despite the Fourth Amendment's guarantee against "unreasonable searches and seizures."

Back in 1995, a Sam Wardlow, standing in front of a house where drug trafficking admittedly went on, saw four patrol cars come around the corner. Even though he wasn't trafficking at that moment himself, he instinctively got into high gear in the opposite direction. That was enough for the police; they chased him down, frisked him, and busted him for having a loaded weapon without a permit. State judges first ruled that, hey, a person's got a right to jog away from police cars just because he doesn't like police cars. "The Constitution gives people a 'right to move along,'" they said. But in a 5-4 ruling, Supreme Court chief justice William Rehnquist said no. "A person's 'nervous, evasive behavior' is one factor that might justify a stop. 'Headlong flight is the consummate act of evasion' and certainly gives a police officer suspicion that something is wrong," he said.

Well, you know, this recent story plays right into the hands, or fears, of a person who might look with trepidation at the message we hear coming from the lips of this first angel found in Revelation 14. There are three mighty angels here in this mysterious book of prophecy. In my Adventist denomination our Bible study groups sometimes get together and discuss "The Three Angels' Messages." And as we've explored so far, that first angel is actually US. People like you and me, who accept God's challenge to us to share the "everlasting gospel" with our friends and neighbors.

But now we come to verse seven together, and right away shades of "Illinois vs. Wardlow" and scampering away from police paddy wagons come to mind. Here it is: "He [that first angel, those who proclaim the gospel message] said in a loud voice, 'Fear God and give Him glory, because the hour of His judgment has come. Worship Him who made the heavens, the earth, the sea and the springs of water.'"

That's quite a message, isn't it? "Fear God." In fact, all through the Bible we kind of find that as a recurring theme: "Thunder-from-Sinai. Fear God." Especially in the Old Testament, those two words come booming down over and over. "Fear God." Maybe you remember in the book of Proverbs – in fact, it's in the very first chapter, right up front – these well-known words: "The fear of the Lord is the beginning of wisdom."

Of course here in Revelation 14 – and we have to admit it, even if we're soldiers in the Lord's army – these words "Fear God" kind of hit us like a cop car coming around the corner. Especially when the rest of the verse explicitly says: " . . . Because the hour of His judgment has come."

Not only is that police car coming in our direction, but the red light is on, the billy clubs are out, the tear gas is ready, the handcuffs are gleaming in the moonlight, and we even see the judge in the back seat, ready to sentence us to 50 years in solitary. Or, in this case, HELL. So you and I, along with Sam Wardlow, might say, "Fear God indeed. I'm running! I'm going in the other direction. I'm going to duck down a back alley and hide over on Atheist Avenue."

Well, let's slow down for a moment. First of all, if you and I, as Christians, are actually, in a sense, helping give this message, we want to analyze what we're doing. Are we out to scare our neighbors into running away from this almighty God who's strapping on His sword of vengeance? Is that the message we want to participate in sharing?

Let's return to the realization that this angel – meaning all Christians who share the gospel – are proclaiming to the entire planet . . . what? It says right here: "The everlasting gospel." Never forget: the gospel is good news! It's wonderful news! It's the best news! I like to suggest that it's basically two words long: JESUS SAVES! And everything else we say about God, about "fear," and about "the hour of His judgment" has to be linked to this understanding that the everlasting gospel is absolutely the best news in the world. That Jesus is in it. That the salvation He offers is in it.

Henry Feyerabend, who inspires hope in the hearts of so many viewers in Canada who enjoy his *It Is Written* TV programs up there, has written a commentary book called *Revelation Verse By Verse*. And he says this about the good news, or "everlasting gospel": "The everlasting gospel never changes. There is only ONE gospel."

And he cites Romans 1:16, 17 for us. The Apostle Paul tells us: "I am not ashamed of the gospel, because it is the power of God for the salvation of everyone who believes: first for the Jew, then for the Gentile. For in the gospel a righteousness from God is revealed, a righteousness that is by faith from first to last, just as it is written: 'The righteous [or just] will live by faith.'"

Paul says to us, "Hey, the gospel is good news! I'm not ashamed to tell it." Let me tell you something. If God were someone to really be afraid of, if the threats of judgment meant that any sane person would run down a dark street, into a dark building, and hide under the bed . . . there's no way I would want to be part of a radio team preaching about that kind of God. I *would* be ashamed to preach a message of "fear," if fear means terror and fleeing and "Illinois vs. Wardlow." But Paul says that the gospel is about our salvation. And about God's power being available to help us, not lock us up.

It's also about a kind of righteousness that comes by faith, or by trusting in Jesus. NOT by striving in our own power to accomplish human perfection. So Paul says: "This is good news. I'm not ashamed of it!" In fact, over in Galatians 1:8, he goes on to say: "But even if we or an angel from heaven should preach a gospel other than the one we preached to you, let him be eternally condemned!"

Henry Feyerabend then continues along this line of "one everlasting gospel": "[It] was first announced in Eden." And he points us to Genesis 3:15, where God promises Adam and Eve, who just sinned, that He would send a Redeemer. To do what? To save them! By the third chapter of the Bible, here are those two words: JESUS SAVES! Adam and Eve were hiding, cowering in the bushes, ashamed. Just like this Mr. Wardlow. Sure that God would frisk them and reject them and hate them and put handcuffs on them. But what does He tell them? "Jesus saves. My own Son saves; I'll send Him to save you."

Henry Feyerabend again: "[The same gospel was then announced] to the children of Israel." And he cites as proof Hebrews 4:2, where Paul, writing about the Hebrew nation, tells us: "For we also have had the gospel preached to us, just as they did."

Then Henry's concluding line about this everlasting gospel: "And it is proclaimed anew in every generation. It meets the needs of every crisis in the world's history."

So here are two things for us to hold onto. First of all, this gospel, this good news, this two-word proclamation – JESUS SAVES! – is never-changing, from the first Eden to the restored Eden. From Adam down to me, and from Eve down to you and your kids and grandkids. JESUS SAVES.

But now, what about this "fear"? The Bible does say that; there's no doubt.

Did you know, though, that in the Greek - and you'll find this beautiful nuance throughout the Bible - the word is *phobeo?* And it basically means: "to reverence." One Bible commentary makes this inspired observation: "Used here not in the sense of being afraid of God, but in the sense of coming to Him with reverence and awe. It conveys the thought of absolute loyalty to God, of full surrender to His will."

So you and I are not to be afraid of God. Absolutely not. Angels are always saying to human beings – to the Christmas shepherds in the fields, and the rest of us too – "Fear not!" The arrival of God is good news. Jesus even came to our world as a seven-pound, two-ounce *baby* . . . just to make sure we wouldn't be afraid of Him. But we DO need to reverence God. We do need to take seriously the announcement of these three angels: "Fear God and give glory to Him." Because this is a last-day invitation. God, the friendly Judge, wants to rule in our favor, but there aren't many days left in which to *choose* Him as our friendly Judge.

And as we always like to say on the radio: "TODAY'S the best day to do that."

4

JUMPING ON THE BED

It's probably the most famous – or infamous – jumping-on-the-bed story since Bill Cosby's childhood confessions from four decades ago. In recent years there has been gossip galore about visitors to the White House who, for a generous contribution to the President's reelection fund, were given the privilege of sleeping in the Lincoln Bedroom. But the story that broke the camel's back was about a Hollywood actress named Markie Post, and fellow Clinton supporter Linda Bloodworth-Thomason. Not only were the two White House guests staying in the Executive Mansion . . . they were also jumping up and down on the bed in the Lincoln Bedroom.

Well, I'm sure there are many, many told and untold stories about the silly goings-on at 1600 Pennsylvania Avenue. In a *Voice of Prophecy* program in December of 1999 lamenting the loss of John F. Kennedy, Jr. in that plane crash, we shared the story where little three-year-old John-John called his daddy a "foo-foo head." And the Chief Executive of our nation looked at him with mock sternness: "John," he scolded, "you cannot call the President of the United States of America a foo-foo head!" And we smile at that one. But the image of two grown women giddily jumping on the bed where President Abraham Lincoln, who freed the slaves and gave this reunited country the Gettysburg Address, used to rest after a day of binding up the nation's wounds . . . well, it did not sit well with many Americans.

Peggy Noonan, former speechwriter for the Reagan White House, wrote a scolding article in the *Reader's Digest,* pointing out that these people had lost all sense of decorum. You simply don't do that. It doesn't show proper respect for the office, for the heritage of greatness that ought to reside in that grand old house.

Well, this gets back to a King James-sounding expression from Chapter Three. As we think about the powerful warning message of these three angels "flying in the midst of heaven" here in Revelation chapter 14, that first angel begins by saying to the world: "Fear God. Fear God and give glory to Him." The point not being that people should shrink away in terror from God, but that they should have a proper respect for Him. An awe that is comfortable – if you know God and are in relationship with Him – but an awe that is still very real, very life-changing.

Born-again Christian Chuck Colson, who used to walk the halls of power and sit in the inner sanctum, and who probably put his feet up on the furniture with his boss, Richard Nixon, saw both the hallowed side and the seamy side. He finally went to jail, partly because he, too, didn't fully appreciate the need to respect the gravity of where he was. This was the White House! This was a place for truth, and for justice, and for integrity. He does write how, most of the time, visitors who came into the Oval Office – some of them planning to "tell old Nixon a thing or two" – generally got very quiet when they realized that this was The Place. This was where the power and authority were.

What does it mean to "fear" God in the sense that we reverence Him? First of all, we recognize Him for who He is. And one of the big points of these "Three Angels' Messages" is to remind us that God the Father is our Creator. "Worship Him who made the heavens, the earth, the sea and the springs of water."

We'll return to that concept later, but this is one reason why we OWE God our reverence. He made us! Just because of that, we would owe Him. Now, God has done so much more for us than to simply jump-start our existences, but it begins there. We fear and reverence God because He made this universe by His own spoken word. He is our Creator, our Designer, our Maker . . . and so we ought not to "jump on the bed," especially in His presence.

It's interesting that one of the world's greatest kings, a man who himself commanded respect and power and authority, mirrors almost word for word the message of these three angels. King Solomon, after years of careless living, of partying in his own White House with call girls and presidential interns, pushes it all to the side and comes to his senses. At the very end of his memoirs, which we know as the Bible book of Ecclesiastes, he has this to say for our edification: "Now all has been heard; here is the conclusion of the matter: Fear God and keep His commandments, for this is the whole duty of man. For God will bring every deed into judgment, including every hidden thing, whether it is good or evil."

Notice Solomon's two conclusions as to WHY we should respect God. First of all, because He has called His followers to obey. "Respect God and obey Him," he says. And you know, as we explore more closely these three angel messages in Revelation 14, we're going to find that same challenge there: to be obedient to God. To show respect BY obeying, by following Him. Just a few chapters over in Revelation is a fantastic verse describing the people of God in the last generations of time. And the Bible says very simply: "They follow the Lamb wherever He goes."

Every time I read those words, I just want to get on my knees and make this pledge. "Jesus, I'll go wherever You lead me; I'll do whatever You ask me to do. Every day, and every time." Because that's how we show God our respect.

Point number two: these last days are a time for respect because "the hour of His judgment has come." Admittedly, when cop cars squeal toward us with the red lights flashing, most of us are likely to run in the other direction. Because, as they used to say, rather frivolously on *Laugh-In,* "Here comes the judge!" And if judgment is a serious matter, by a serious God, at a serious time in history, then it's a time to be respectful. It's not a time for jumping on beds, or for going our own way.

But now to the all-important question: What kind of judgment is coming up? That is crucial to our study, certainly, because we're told to show respect or biblical "fear" precisely in response to the fact of judgment coming. "Fear God and give glory to Him *because* the hour of His judgment is come." There are those who propose that only the wicked will be judged, or perhaps only those who are living carelessly outside of a relationship with God. Those who are "jumping on the bed," so to speak. It's even suggested that God Himself is somehow on trial here at the end, that He will be "judged on how He judges."

We're actually going to find that the Bible clearly teaches four aspects of judgment, involving different groups, and happening at different times. But King Solomon and these three angels are united in telling us that there most certainly WILL be a judgment scene. And no matter what the details are, when God the Ruler over heaven and earth is involved in any kind of judgment, it is a grand and sober time. A time to look up, not look away. A time to take off your hat, and your shoes, because the ground is holy and God is especially holy.

I like the plain interpretation to be found in the *Clear Word* paraphrase, which is not a Bible, but a marvelous resource for study and reflection. Notice how author Jack Blanco renders this message by the first angel: "Then the scene changed, and I saw an angel flying high in the air, carrying the last message of God's good news to every nation, race, tribe, and language. He called out in a loud voice for everyone to hear, saying, 'Stand in awe of God" – that's good, isn't it? – "and give glory to Him, because the time has come for Him to clear HIS name and to judge the world. Worship Him who made the heavens, the earth, the sea, and the springs of water."

Even Jesus clearly taught about the judgment; you remember the story of the sheep and the goats, for instance. So it is a sober thing, a real thing. But in Matthew 13 He gives us another parable about the judgment: a story about wheat and tares. Good crops with a whole bunch of weeds planted in among them, ruining things, choking everything. And the owner says: "An enemy did this." "What shall we do?" asks the servant. "This is terrible." And the owner says very calmly, still in control: "Leave it all right there. Let them both be for now. Let them both grow. But *in the end*, when it comes time for the harvest, the weeds will be bundled up and destroyed."

So it's serious stuff, isn't it? Notice, though, that the judgment, the bundling-up-and-destroying conclusion, happens at the end of time. So judgment is a last-day experience. That's why these three angels are a last-day phenomenon, a spiritual opportunity for NOW, for you and for me.

But through it all, good news. Because JESUS SAVES.

5

INSTANT VERDICTS FROM THE INTERNET

Here's a Regis Philbin question for all of us to think about. How long would it take for God to learn, or to know, everything there is to know about you? We're familiar with the New Testament promise by Jesus Himself – you'll find it in Matthew 10:30 – that God the Father actually has numbered every hair on your head. I get a kick out of how, in the popular Christian group, the Gaither Vocal Band, Mark Lowry likes to always tease Bill Gaither about how much hair he has . . . or doesn't have. And Bill, being the set-up man for Mark's humor, quotes the verse about God counting every hair. And Mark comes right back: "Yeah, Bill, and God wants to thank you for not taking up too much of His time!"

But wouldn't you agree that God knows INSTANTLY everything there is to know about me, and about you? He knows our names; the Word of God tells us that. He knew us before we were born; the Bible says that too. He knows everything we do, every thought we think.

I was reading not too long ago about computer speeds on the Internet. And of course, the way the computer industry is changing, anything I put in this chapter can make me into a laughing-stock just in the few weeks it takes to go to press. But I understand that college kids, in recent months, have become kind of addicted to what they call the "ethernet." Don't ask me to explain the why's and wherefore's about it all, but apparently many college campuses are wired up with such high-speed modems that the students have INSTANT access to whatever they need. If they log into a web site . . . *Bam!* It's on the screen. Do they want to download a thousand-page book? *Bam!* In about four seconds, the whole book is in their dorm room. Do they want to get the latest pop song by the Cranberries, in MP3 format, downloaded? *Bam!* They're listening to the entire album in about two nanoseconds.

Whole movies? *Bam!* They've got it. There's no waiting around, like the rest of the hackers in the world, while that hourglass thing sits there next to your arrow icon, while the computer thinks . . . and thinks . . . and thinks. On the "ethernet," everything you want, any tidbit of knowledge, any piece of trivia, is just a hundredth of a second away. *Ka-BLAM!* You've got it.

They say – and again, this comes under the heading of "way old news" – that this was one of the huge reasons why AOL and Time Warner recently wanted to merge. Two words: "Swifter connections." America Online's Steve Case wanted those huge cable networks and systems owned by Time Warner, so that instead of just college kids enjoying the immediacy, the *Bam!*, of instant downloading, all of us could start paying AOL for lightning-quick knowledge too.

Well, why bring up the issue of instant knowledge? Here in verse seven, the first angel tells us: "Fear God, and give glory to Him; for the hour of His judgment has come."

And when the Bible talks about the judgment of God, every citizen on planet earth gets very interested. Or *ought* to get very interested. Because first of all, if God is the judge, there's not going to be anything that slips by Him. Agreed? Secondly, if God is the judge, He's very capable of handing out great rewards, or extremely severe punishments. If He gives you a long sentence, there's not anyplace I know of above Him where you can appeal to get your jail time shortened.

So what's involved here? Are we on the witness seat? Are we on trial? When does it all happen?

In Revelation 20, just six chapters over from where we're studying, it says this about judgment: "And I saw a great white throne, and Him that sat on it, from whose face the earth and the heaven fled away; and there was found no place for them. And I saw the dead, small and great, stand before God; *and the books were opened*."

The book of Psalms talks about these same books in chapter 69, in referring to those who reject God: "Let them be blotted out of the book of the living, and not be written with the righteous."

And maybe some of us, even in the Christian faith, have had a picture of God, or of Jesus working with God, carefully and laboriously going through this incredible, HUGE book . . . a book with six billion people's records in it. In fact, way more than six billion names, because the Bible clearly teaches here that even the dead, anybody who has lived and then died in all the years of earth's history, has a record in heaven's "books."

Can we imagine, you and I, a scenario where God wants to make a decision about whether I should be saved or lost? So He has to look in this huge, huge book: past the A's, and the B's, and the C's, through the H's, and the L's and Q's, and finally to the S's. And then down, down, looking, through the fine print, until He gets to my name. "Smith, David B." And then, maybe with glasses on, He begins to review 45 years of my deeds: good and bad, loving and selfish. Feeding the widows and orphans, or not feeding them. Reflecting the character of Jesus, or not reflecting it. Obeying Him, or not obeying Him. And He looks and studies, and sifts through evidence, and weighs all the factors. "What should I do with David Smith?" Maybe it's a close call: 51% to 49%. What should He do? Which way should He let the scales tip?

And of course, to study 45 years of a man's behavior patterns might take pretty close to 45 years, if you review the entire record. Multiply that by six billion trial cases, and we can see why it might be a rather long court session.

Well, I think the evidence is clear, on the other hand, that the incredible mind of God is somewhat like that "ethernet." How well does He know me? Perfectly! And how long would it take for Him to "download" every pertinent detail about my entire life? It would be instantaneous, wouldn't it? It would be ludicrous to think that with God there would be that waiting time, like when your computer kind of gurgles and makes that rumbly sound while the program you want slowly, slowly, slowly boots up.

There's a wonderful old book entitled The *Knowledge of the Holy* by the late A. W. Tozer. He's talking about our knowledge of God, but there's a chapter entitled "The Divine Omniscience" about HIS knowledge. Keep in mind what all this would imply about how long it would take, or how hard it would be, for God to be the Judge of all the earth. "To say that God is omniscient is to say that He possesses perfect knowledge and therefore has no need to learn," he writes. "But it is more: it is to say that God has never learned and cannot learn."

In other words, God will never once say: "Oh, my, I didn't know that." Or, "Oh dear, I don't remember that; I'm going to have to look it up in some book. I'm going to have to log onto AOL and check out that fact, because I don't remember." That's not going to happen. Tozer continues: "The Scriptures teach that God has never learned from anyone. 'Who hath directed the Spirit of the Lord, or being His counsellor hath taught Him?'"

That's from Isaiah 40, a marvelous chapter. But let's up the ante a bit more, still quoting from this book by Pastor Tozer: "He knows all that can be known. And this He knows instantly and with a fullness of perfection that includes every possible item of knowledge concerning everything that exists or could have existed anywhere in the universe at any time in the past or that may exist in the centuries or ages yet unborn. God knows instantly and effortlessly all matter and all matters, all mind and every mind, all spirit and all spirits, all being and every being. . . . He knows no thing better than any other thing, but all things equally well. He never discovers anything. He is never surprised, never amazed. He never wonders about anything nor (except when drawing men out for their own good) does He seek information or ask questions."

Whew! I think it's time to take a deep breath! You talk about the "ethernet"; this is the God-Net! INSTANTLY . . . every fact. Every detail. Every thought, every nuance, every piece of information or feeling or emotion or hurt or joy.

This kind of turns on its head the entire question of the judgment. If God is looking into books in heaven, I can tell you this: He's not looking in those books to find out something. This isn't research to Him; He's not looking for an answer He hasn't already got. And if not – if in the Judgment He doesn't need to study our case, or think about or ponder our case – then He must be doing all of this for some other reason. Or for some other people.

Keep reading, and we'll begin to think about who those people might be.

6

THE VERDICT IN 27 A.D.

It was a three-hour piece of celluloid fiction, but it didn't lessen the horror of the outcome. An innocent man was about to die in the electric chair. And not just an innocent man, but a quiet, gentle man who had in him God's gift of tender healing.

And the main guard on the "green mile" knew in his heart that John Coffey – "like the drink, but not spelled the same" – was innocent. He had committed no crime; on the contrary, he had tried to use his spiritual gift of healing to save the two little girls someone else had killed. Now *he* was about to sit down in "Old Sparky."

And in a moment of spiritual fear the guard confesses to his wife: "I've done some things I'm not proud of, but this is the first time I ever felt really actually in danger of hell." Why? Because how could he possibly face God on Judgment Day and have an answer when God asked him: "Why did you kill one of My gifts?"

Paul Edgecombe knew that a judgment was about to take place there on Death Row, and that it would be wrong. It was inescapable; night after night he had tried to think of a way to fix this great wrong. But there was no way out. An innocent man was going to pay the price of a guilty one. A gentle, good person was going to be treated as a vile criminal, and at the stroke of midnight, "ride the lightning."

It's interesting that even in a Stephen King thriller like this, mankind is sobered by the specter of Judgment Day. Because we know in our hearts that God will not get things wrong. He will make no mistakes. And this fictional prison guard, Paul Edgecombe, rightly admitted his fear. He was literally afraid of hell, because he would have no answer for the probing questions from the throne.

Here in the *Los Angeles Times*, the wonderful columnist Mike
Downey recently reminded us about some real stories of men who
almost got up to the electric chair, or the lethal injection gurney . . .
and then were found to be innocent. Lawrence Marshall, a law
professor at Northwestern University, got a man named Gary
Gauger off death row, proving he had not killed his parents. He
got Rolando Cruz off after ten years on death row. Another man
confessed to killing a little ten-year-old girl, and DNA eventually
proved that Cruz was innocent . . . but ten *years*! Maybe you've
heard how "Hurricane" Carter, the boxer, got out of prison after 20
years of false imprisonment. Here on earth, where police in the
Rampart scandal make mistakes, and where prosecutors might
have racially motivated vendettas to pursue, and where judges are
not infallible – good people go to jail and bad ones roam the
streets. Guilty men ride in limousines and innocent ones have the
lethal injection needle – "The Spike" – stuck in their veins at 12:01
in the morning.

Here again is the very heart of "The Three Angels' Messages,"
"Then I saw another angel" – actually, this is the first of the three
– "flying in mid-air, and he had the eternal gospel to proclaim to
those who live on the earth – to every nation, tribe, language and
people. He said in a loud voice, 'Fear God because the hour of
His judgment has come.'"

This concept of the judgment is, and ought to be, a sober one.
First of all, it's a life-or-death time for every single person. There
won't be any appeal beyond this judgment. What's more, those
who are involved will be facing a Judge who knows perfectly and
absolutely and instantly what really happened. That's why this fictional jail guard, Paul Edgecombe, was so shaken in his soul. He
knew that God knew! God knew every motive, every thought,
every detail about this tragedy.

The Bible talks very openly and in detailed fashion about the Judgment. I don't believe it's a metaphor, or just colorful, apocryphal writing. "Books were opened," says the Word of God. The Judge is seated on His throne.

But here's some good news found in a great, scholarly book by a seminary professor named Dr. Norman Gulley. He has a book that describes a lot about what the Bible teaches about the Judgment, and there's one sentence I want to give you right here: "The pre-Advent judgment is *wonderful* news for all good Christians." You might be wondering about that expression: "The pre-Advent judgment." That simply means that when Jesus comes again, at the Second Coming, He already knows who He is going to save. That makes sense, doesn't it? In fact, the book of Revelation teaches this in almost the very last verse. Chapter 22, verse 12: "Behold, I come quickly; and My reward is with Me, to give every man according as his work shall be."

Very clearly, if Jesus comes again in the clouds, as He promised many times He would do, He's already decided who are His. He has pre-judged His trophies. "I am the Shepherd, and I know My sheep," He said in the Gospels.

If you are His, if you have given your life to Him and accepted His gift at Calvary and are living in relationship with Him right now ... He knows that fact! And He's judged IN YOUR FAVOR already! No wonder Dr. Gulley writes that the Judgment is marvelous news for any Christian. And Christ promises: "Based on that Judgment in your favor, I'm coming with a reward for you." And what a reward, by the way!

Again, there are really four judgment scenes in the Word of God. We want to look at all four of them, but I kind of like what this same seminary teacher, Dr. Gulley, says on the next page. "Judgment Day was primarily and initially at Calvary. Jesus said of the cross, 'NOW is the time for judgment on this world; NOW the prince of this world will be driven out.'"

That's John 12:31, a tremendous, pivotal verse. And really, he's absolutely right. At Calvary, God was judged victorious and Lucifer was judged to be wrong and defeated and destroyed. Not destroyed YET . . . but destined for destruction.

And if we accept the victory judgment at Calvary in our lives now – God knows that! He knows it instantly! And He rejoices in judging in our favor.

But we need also to consider the timing of the Judgment. True indeed – the real Judgment happened at Calvary, and we all praise God for the results. Jesus is vindicated, Lucifer condemned. However, that only has implications for you and me if we accept Calvary, if we allow the death of Jesus Christ to cover over our guilt. So there certainly is a sense where judgment for us happens much later than 27 A.D. In fact, the book of Hebrews, chapter 9, makes it clear what happens in our own case, each one of us: "He [Christ] has appeared once for all at the end of the age to do away with sin by the sacrifice of Himself. Just as man is destined to die once, and after that to face judgment."

As long as you are alive, your eternal destiny is an open question. Will you accept the Cross and be declared innocent? Or will you, by your own choice, reject that Cross and remain in guilt? Even on a deathbed, even hanging on a cross like that thief next to Jesus, even with just moments left, a person might choose this Teacher from Galilee to be their Savior . . . and live forever.

Again, let's recognize that our wonderful, omniscient God, who is so eager to save each one of us, would know immediately, instantly, if a man or woman had chosen Him. That's no mystery to God; He doesn't have to look up your name on some CD-ROM reference library. He doesn't have to pore over page after page of transcripts to see if you have more good deeds than bad ones. He KNOWS – He's always known – if you or I have really and truly cast our fates at the foot of the Cross. He knows it . . . and it takes less than two seconds for Him to know it. GOD really doesn't need a Judgment process. Because He knows.

In that sad miscarriage of justice on the "green mile," prison guard Paul Edgecombe slowly, painfully, found out the things the jury didn't know. The hidden secrets the prosecutors had missed. But truth doesn't trickle into God's courtroom. He knows.

So the WHO of the Judgment, and the TIMING of the Judgment . . . must involve others besides God. But who might that be?

7

WHO WANTS TO KNOW?

Have you ever heard of *eldils*? Or *macrobes*? In the mysterious,
galactic worlds created in the science-fiction trilogy by the late
Christian writer C. S. Lewis, *eldils* was really a word for angels.
Holy beings – some of them in heaven, but others who were
assigned to various planets and stars in God's vast universe.
Macrobes were the dark angels, fallen angels, who were bent on
taking over *Thulcandra*, or "The Silent Planet" . . . meaning earth.

And there were other beings. If you read the first book in the trilogy, *Out of the Silent Planet*, this man named Elwin Ransom is kid-
napped and taken to *Malacandra* – or Mars. And there he finds
several kinds of rational creatures: the *Hrossa*, the *Sorns*. These
weren't human, but on a par with them: other kinds of intelligent
beings capable of speech, reading, writing, thinking spiritual
thoughts, etc.

And in a sense, the whole battle of sin, of Good versus Evil, happening down in our world, was something they were all watching.
They knew about God, of course. To serve Him was the obvious
thing; not one of them had ever thought of doing anything else.
They all knew about Maleldil, His Son. Even a secular reader
soon figures out that's Jesus. And how Maleldil went down to
Thulcandra, the silent planet, the one place that is somehow isolat-
ed, quarantined, so that He could perhaps rescue that one lost
world.

Well, it's marvelous reading, and filled with Bible truth from first
to last. But the incredible insight is this. You and I and Adam and
Eve and all of this lost human race are down here. Jesus, the Son
of God, is born down here. Calvary happens down here. The plan
of redemption is happening down here. And in these three admittedly fiction books, it's suggested that all of these UNfallen worlds

out there are quietly watching. Sin isn't just a mess, but a mysterious mess. They haven't tasted it; they don't understand it. All they know is righteousness and peace and happiness, and so the causes of sin, the results of sin, are something they can only scratch their heads about from a great, great distance.

In fact, in the first book, this Ransom, the man from earth, has to painfully explain to the citizens of *Malacandra* what things like war and murder are. What prostitution is. And the people there just shake their heads in confusion.

But in studying about the Judgment, you and I have been kind of scratching our own heads about the fact that God knows every single fact in the universe instantly. The "hard drive" of His divine mind has so many giga-gigabytes that He just knows. So why does He need to open up books and examine evidence and have a "Judgment"? If He knows our hearts and minds, instantly, and if He knows if we truly do or do not have a Calvary relationship with His Son, then make a decision and be done with it. Two seconds: finished.

Well, I believe that this space trilogy is a huge reason why there is a Judgment, and why it does take longer than two seconds. In the final analysis, I don't think *Out of the Silent Planet* IS fiction. Our heavenly Father, Creator of the universe – and I really believe this – has those silent watchers on many, many worlds. And they are all watching to see how this war turns out.

Have you ever read the very beginnings of the book of Job? Right in chapter one, the King James Version says this: "Now there came a day when the sons of God came to present themselves before the Lord, and Satan came also among them."

Here is a council meeting being held in heaven, and who are the invited board members? The "sons of God." Remember that Adam is called in the New Testament genealogy a "son of God."

That's in Luke three. The leader of this world, until he forfeited that position. Is it possible that God, whose creative power is unlimited, didn't stop with inhabiting just one world, but that He made many of them? And put a king and queen, an Adam and Eve, in charge of each one? That's the scenario, by the way, in C. S. Lewis' second book in the trilogy, *Perelandra* ...a fantastic book about the battle between good and evil, God and Lucifer.

Well, the Bible gives us this hint. I can't give nearly as much weight to a loose paraphrase like the *Clear Word*, by Dr. Jack Blanco, but listen to how he interprets Job 1:6: "In heaven the representatives of other planets in God's created universe came together regularly to meet with Him. One day Satan also came with them and presented himself for admittance. He came to accuse God of being partial to Job." And here's verse 7, just for interest's sake: "God said to Satan, 'On what basis do you want to attend this meeting?' The Accuser answered, 'I represent the planet Earth and have been in charge there for a long time.'"

So is it possible that there are men and women – Adams and Eves from great, sinless societies throughout the universe – who have been watching the Calvary saga on earth with great interest? Well, we don't know that for sure. But let me pose a more down-to-earth question. Aren't there many billions of angels in God's kingdom, still loyal to God, who might have questions about salvation? Lucifer went about heaven with his lies and managed to seduce away a third of the angel forces. You can read about that right here in Revelation, just a couple of pages earlier in chapter 12. But even though the two-thirds group stayed loyal to God, remained in His service, might the accusations from Satan – notice the Bible specifically calls him The Accuser – have stuck in their minds? Is God fair in how He handles this mysterious cancer called sin?

So this is a partial answer to the question we've been asking. The Judgment is actually for those looking on. Angels. Beings on other worlds. And beings on THIS world. If Adolph Hitler was in heaven, would you be interested in finding out how in the world he got in the front gate? If Timothy McVeigh, who carefully planned and then bombed to bits 168 innocent victims, were to call a press conference there on Death Row at Terre Haute, Indiana, and tell reporters: "Surprise! I've found God; I've accepted the Christian message," would you have questions about whether he should get a mansion in heaven? And how big a mansion? Would you want to know? Wouldn't the families of victims in Oklahoma City especially want to know?

I found an interesting observation in one of the classic old books people read in my Adventist denomination. It's entitled *The Great Controversy Between Christ and Satan*, and it's filled with discussions about these very issues of "who is watching the great war." And the author, E. G. White, makes this suggestion about the Judgment: "In the great day of final atonement and investigative judgment, the only cases considered are those of the professed people of God."

And maybe we're not sure what to make of that, until we realize something. There are those who have lived on planet earth who openly and unequivocally have said NO to God. "I will not have Him as Ruler of my life," they said. Calvary and salvation were not something they wanted; sin was not something they acknowledged to be a reality in their life.

Of course, God knows that. Instantly, as we've been saying. He knows who are His, and He knows, with regret, those who are not His. And it's safe to say that the watching universe knows about those who have specifically turned their backs on the kingdom of heaven. There's no need to sift evidence in those cases, because they are so open-and-shut.

But . . . then there's us. You, maybe. You've claimed that you're a Christian. But are you really? "Look at that person!" Satan shrieks to anyone who will listen. "They keep sinning! I got 'em 40 times last week." And the watching universe wonders: "Hmmm. Has this person really accepted Calvary? They say so, but talk is cheap. Should they be allowed into heaven for all eternity? And if so, on what basis?"

I might get to heaven, and be so grateful to be there. But as I look around, I can't help but notice a gap. Mr. Jones – or let's say Pastor Jones – of course he should be up here! But he's not. And I say to my accompanying angel: "But . . . but . . . he preached every weekend! He was tremendous! His sermons were masterpieces. He talked about God incessantly! How in the world can he not be in the Kingdom of heaven?" And even though God doesn't need to look through a whole lot of books to make the right decision about Pastor Jones, all at once I'D like to examine those books line by line by line.

It reminds me of that Old Testament scenario where Abraham, one of God's best friends and defenders, looked right at his Maker and said: "Will not the Judge of all the earth do right?"

Let's look again at that alternate rendition of this "first angel's message" which goes like this: "Stand in awe of God and give glory to Him, because the time as come for Him to clear HIS name and to judge the world."

And if Timothy McVeigh is standing on the sea of glass, and Pastor Jones isn't, clearing His own name in the Judgment might be the very first thing God has to do.

8

EXPOSING THE HYPOCRITES

There was a rotten little story in the Ventura County section of my hometown paper, the *Los Angeles Times*. And really, this story is just one of hundreds I could pick from. The article was about statutory rape: older men who have sex with young girls. Which, as we all know, is a crime. This one example was of a teen-aged girl named Carrie, age 16. There was a teacher at her school; he was 31. And the two of them began to drift into conversations that were inappropriately intimate. Pretty soon he was kissing her. Then, after the summer break, they picked up where they left off, and soon this married man was having an affair with a high school junior. She had to "sneak around" to be with him, lying to her friends and her own family. "I really, really cared for him," she confessed later. "I really didn't see what was happening until it had happened."

Stories like that are probably a dime a dozen these days, unfortunately. But here's the hidden half of the tale. Carrie was attending a private Christian school. And the 31-year-old teacher she had the affair with was the religion teacher at the school. This was the man who was teaching the Bible classes, who stood up in front of Carrie's classroom and gave her training and instruction in Scriptural principles . . . and then met her later for the illicit tête-à-tête.

Of course this is terrible – but no more terrible than the sins of pride and selfishness and anger that you and I indulge in. We're very tempted to think that Seventh Commandment violations are the most wicked ones, as well as the most exciting. But the point we ought to really think about is linked to what we've just been considering.

The Bible tells us, here in this study passage of Revelation chapter 14, that we are to be of sober minds in these last days. "Fear God

and give glory to Him, for the hour of His judgment has come."
And we've halted our expedition right here for a few chapters to
meditate together about what this judgment is really all about.

In reviewing, notice that this end-time judgment, sometimes called
the Pre-Advent Judgment because it happens right before Jesus
returns, basically involves two groups: real Christians and those
who *claim* to be Christians. Again we rejoice over the "sound
bite" from Dr. Norman Gulley's book, *Christ Is Coming!*: "The
pre-Advent judgment is wonderful news for all good Christians."

But now we think about this Bible teacher, who says with his
mouth: "I am a Christian." He teaches and preaches from the
Word of God; he allows himself to be set up as a role model for
impressionable young people. He is a professing Christian. But
then with his life, with his after-hour liaisons and his midnight ren-
dezvous, he seems to give testimony that his profession of the
Christian faith is simply that: a profession. Just words. Is it possible, then, that the judgment scenes described in the Bible, by Jesus
in the Gospels and again here in Revelation 14, are for the purpose
of deciding who is really with God and who is simply pretending
to be with Him?

We could really stay out of the book of Revelation entirely, and
just read the great parables of Jesus, and still learn many powerful
truths about the Judgment. In Matthew chapter 25 is the famous
parable by Christ about the ten virgins who were going to a wedding. Five wise, and five foolish . . . remember? All of them professed to be friends of the groom; all of them claimed that they
were in the wedding party. But in verse 12, the groom – that
would be Jesus Himself, of course – says through a locked door, to
the five foolish ones: "Hey, I don't know you. You say we're
friends, but we're not. You weren't prepared with the extra oil in
case I came late."

Just back a few pages from there, in Matthew 22, is another parable along the same lines. There's a great wedding banquet put on by the King for His Son . . . and you can certainly figure out that part. God the Father and Jesus, of course. And they invite all sorts of people: good ones and bad ones. Rich and poor. Nicely dressed and not-so-nicely dressed. But the king graciously provides all of those in attendance with a free wedding garment.

However, one man sitting at Table #7, sampling the caviar and enjoying the free food, doesn't have on that free garment. He's right there with the king's friends; he's a professed part of the entourage. But he doesn't have on the requisite clothing. And the king judges him on that basis; he has this rebellious man sent away, "into the darkness, where there will be weeping and gnashing of teeth."

I've already mentioned the famous "weed" story, back in Matthew 13, where there's a certain field. Wheat is in the field, and weeds are there too. There should be only wheat, of course, but somehow the tares and briars are there as well. "Hey, let's get rid of these," says a servant. "They don't belong here." But the owner very wisely responds: "No, that's all right. If we pull up the weeds right now, we might uproot the wheat with it. Leave it all right there. But when it comes time for the harvest, I'll sort it all out. The wheat will go into the barn, and the weeds will be destroyed." And for the third time, we find this imagery where the real and the professed real are all together. God doesn't disturb the mix; He doesn't separate the genuine article from the hypocrite. Not then. But in the end, when it really counts, then He makes a determination about it all; He separates the good from the pretend good. Of course, a wise farmer with a keen eye might know very quickly which plants are wheat and which ones are tares. But is it possible that He would very carefully and even methodically explain to the servants: "Okay, these are fine. These are good plants. The ones right over there, you can tell by the leaves, and by those tiny jagged edges – see, right there? – those are the weeds"? Would He open up the judgment process so that everyone who works at the farm understands how He makes His decisions? Would He, in a sense, "put it in the *L.A. Times*"?

Let me say it again. God already knows who are His. And He knows it instantly. If you and I are able to spot hypocrisy – and most of us think we're pretty good at it – you can be sure that God knows in a heartbeat if someone is just talking and not doing. At that Christian high school, He knows a fake Bible teacher from a real one. But I believe this judgment process talked about in Revelation 14 is for the benefit of the watching universe. It's for the angels. It's for you and me, involving the cases where maybe we don't know a person's heart.

Actually, Jesus addresses this issue, not in a parable, but right out on the street corner, so to speak. In His well-known Sermon on the Mount, which run from Matthew five to Matthew seven, He says a few words about people like this womanizing Bible teacher: "Not everyone who says to me, 'Lord, Lord,' will enter the king-dom of heaven, but only he who *does the will* of my Father who is in heaven. Many will say to Me on that day, 'Lord, Lord, did we not prophesy in Your name, and in Your name drive out demons and perform many miracles?' Then I will tell them plainly, 'I never knew you. Away from me, you evildoers!'"

I suppose at this point, you might be tempted the same way I sometimes am. Maybe by now "sober" has just plain turned into raw fear. "There's no chance for me," you say. "I've said I love God. I've said I want to serve Him. But I've messed up so many times, I'm probably in the same camp as the guy at that school who cheated on his wife. Or like the five foolish virgins. 'Cause I TALK a lot better than I DO. You say the Judgment is 'wonderful news for all good Christians,' but I'm not a very good Christian." Which means that if God and Jesus are up in heaven and going through the books, with a lot of angels looking on to see if we're hypocrites . . . well, that sounds like bad news.

I hear what you're saying. Believe me. And just because you're *reading* these pages, and I'm *writing* them, doesn't mean we don't both have a lot of weeds in our hearts. But let me remind you right here that the Apostle Paul bemoaned how he was the worst sinner around. He reeked of hypocrisy and bad thoughts; he was steeped in naughty attitudes. And yet, he calls the gospel "good news." Good news for him. Good news for the thief on the cross. Good news for me. Good news for you.

So don't let go of the rope just yet.

9

ST. NICK'S WAY OF JUDGING

I know Christmas is still a ways off, but every December we sing a certain song that has to do with the Judgment. Not in church, probably, because the lyrics go like this: "You'd better watch out. You'd better not cry. You'd better not pout; I'm telling you why." And then the apocalyptic warning: "Santa Claus is coming to town."

And on what basis is old Saint Nick going to judge the human race? Is grace mentioned? Is forgiveness found in the chorus? Does this Christmas song explain to us that relationship is the important thing, and that if you wait up on Christmas Eve until midnight, and if you love Santa Claus, that is all he expects? No, it doesn't seem to work that way. Here are the guidelines, and we all know them: "He's making a list, And checking it twice. Going to find out who's naughty or nice. Santa Claus is coming to town."

And you know, the legalism gets even worse. "He sees you when you're sleeping. He knows when you're awake. He knows if you've been bad or good. So be good for goodness' sake."

Let me say something right here. I'm awfully glad that "Santa Claus Is Coming to Town" is NOT an expression of the Christian message! I'm glad that born-again Christians don't have to be any more afraid of the Judgment at the end of time than they do the arrival of the sleigh and reindeer on the rooftop. We've been saying for about five chapters now: "The Judgment before Jesus comes is wonderful news for the born-again believer!"

Furthermore, we've said on the radio for the past seven decades that the BASIS of our salvation doesn't have to do if we've been good or bad. Doesn't have to do with if we've been naughty or nice. Doesn't have to do with the positive or negative deeds on the list that God makes and then checks twice. We're saved in heaven because we've accepted the blood of Jesus Christ, which He shed on Calvary. Isn't that tremendous news?

And yet . . . and yet . . . as we study what that Word of God teaches about the Judgment, do you know something? We find even Jesus telling us – not exactly word for word – but certainly *shades* of this very Christmas song: "Santa Claus Is Coming to Town." We find a list. We find God checking it twice – in fact, maybe up to four times. We find naughty and nice. Good and bad. Saints getting presents, and sinners not getting them.

In Matthew 26 Jesus tells one of His most well-known "Judgment parables." It's entitled "The Sheep and the Goats." The returning King – that's Jesus Himself – separates people into these two groups: Sheep and Goats. One group on His right, the other on the left. And on what basis are people separated that way? Well, one group does certain things: feeding the hungry, giving someone a drink, inviting in the stranger, clothing the destitute, visiting the sick, ministering to someone in prison. One, two, three, four, five, six . . . THINGS you could do, or not do. Six things that might equally appear on Santa Claus' list, or on Almighty God's. In fact, when you get down to verse 41, which is about the lost people, the "goats," it's the same six things again. These folks did NOT feed the hungry, visit the prisons, etc. And we all recall the great line: "Inasmuch as ye did it NOT to one of the least of these, ye did it not to Me."

Well, this is Judgment. And it's not on the basis of grace, or of relationship. It's on the basis of a Christmas list: good deeds or NO good deeds. What do we make of this?

If we move away from what we thought were the warm-and-fuzzy Gospels, and come back to our study book of Revelation, the announcement about Judgment gets even more forceful. Here's

one of the last verses in the whole Bible: Revelation 22:12:
"Behold, I am coming soon! My reward is with Me, and I will
give to everyone *according to what he has done*."
And just three verses later is a tight little list of types of sinners
who will NOT be in the Kingdom: "Satanic magicians, murderers,
the immoral, idolaters," etc. And we almost hear the familiar tune:
"Makin' a list, and checkin' it twice. Gonna find out who's
naughty or nice."

Again, this kind of Bible discovery can shake a Christian's faith.
Our assurance can evaporate overnight, if we think God is going to
judge us, not on the basis of Calvary, but on the basis of our
behavior. Is everything lost? On top of all this, the Bible tells so
many stories about people who did tons of good deeds. They said
prayers. They used the name of Jesus in church. They worked
mighty miracles. They paid tithe, not just on their paychecks, but
on the tomato plants out in their gardens. And Christ the Judge
says to them: "Get away from Me. I never knew you." So what in
the world is going on here?

Well, it's too vital a Bible pillar of truth to fit into a simple story,
but let me try anyway. Imagine that God invites you to become a
friend to His own Son. "Come," He invites. "I want you and My
Son to be friends. He loves you so much . . . and I do too. In fact,
that's your only hope – to be a friend to My Son. I have heavenly
mansions waiting for all of the friends of My Son."

He then also gives us the great news that His own Son is a fantastic driving instructor. Jesus is eager to ride along with us on this
trip through life. Right there in the car with us. Not just enjoying
and savoring the friendship . . . but He'll be right there, willing to
give loving counsel. A Friend's advice. Driving tips. Strategies
and scenarios to avoid the potholes in the road. Ways and means
of avoiding the enemy's misleading road signs he put in your way,
all the confusing arrows pointing in the wrong direction.

And God also promises you that if you get into a friendship, a relationship, with His own Son . . . as time goes by, you'll be a better driver. How could you NOT? Oh, some drivers might progress more than others. Some might make fewer mistakes than others, go the wrong way down one-way streets not as many times – especially the more you're willing to listen to this wonderful Friend in the car with you. But as time goes by, you surely will end up driving up on the curb less often than before. Does that makes sense?

And now, Judgment Day comes. Or, shall we say, the time to get your driver's license. And really, God wants to know just one thing. Actually, as we've been saying, He already knows . . . but the watching universe wants to know just this one thing. Have you got a relationship with the Son? That's it! That's the sum total of it all. Trust in Jesus, or NO trust in Jesus.

Of course, God knows your heart . . . and so it takes Him very little time to determine if you've really entered into that friendship with His Son. He could decide that so easily. But, because there is a host of watching worlds out there, and because the angels would like to know too, God says very simply: "The reality is that those drivers who have been experiencing this relationship and friendship with My Son . . . they don't drive up on the curb so often. They don't mow down pedestrians. They don't get lost and bash up fenders. Not because they're great drivers on their own, but because they've allowed My own Son to help them. So . . . look to see if they're driving on curbs. Or smashing up their cars. Those in relationship with My Son will have a clear pattern . . . *of becoming better drivers*."

So we have a parable about sheep and goats. The ones not in relationship with Christ were the same ones who didn't help their fellow man, who didn't give a cup of cold water. And since some of us onlookers aren't capable of looking at Exhibit A – the inner heart which is in relationship with Jesus – God permits Judgment to also rest on Exhibit B. Which is cups of cold water, and acts of kindness done to strangers . . . as a RESULT OF the fact that Exhibit A – relationship with the Son – is firmly in place.

So I would say to you right here: Take heart! Be ENcouraged, not DIScouraged! Because the eternal question still is this: Are you in a relationship with Jesus? Are you allowing Him to help you drive?

And you say: "But . . . but . . . my driving is still pretty terrible!" Well, don't focus on that. *Are you in relationship*? "But . . . I'm not as kind to others as I wish I was." Don't focus on that. *Are you in relationship*? Are you WILLING for Jesus to make you kinder? Are you asking your best Friend to make you kinder? As He lovingly prompts you to do a kind deed, are you willing to try? And if you fail to follow a prompting today, do you fall on your knees and ask Him to help you tomorrow with another chance?

I have it on good authority that this wonderful Friend uncomplainingly rides through a lot of fender-benders and wrong-way streets . . . as long as you invite him – sincerely – if you invite Him and MEAN it, to stay in the car and help you drive.

And with Him there in the car with you, you're going to pass that driver's test.

10

WHO CAN WE BLAME WORLD WAR I ON?

Have you ever watched a war picture on television, or maybe a documentary on A&E or The History Channel . . . and wanted to just weep at the stupidity of it all? Maybe a Civil War dramatization, where the two sides, the Blue and the Gray, just lined up in a field and went right against each other. Bullets tearing into the wall of flesh, cannonballs mowing down whole clumps of humanity that used to be husbands and fathers and brothers and sons. And it curdles your blood, the sick evil that is represented by this mad thing called war. They say the first 25 minutes of Steven Spielberg's *Saving Private Ryan* is probably the cinematic epitome of slaughter. Wave after wave after wave of men just mowed down by German machine-gun fire as they tried to stagger up Omaha Beach, June 6, 1944.

And maybe you're like me. You think to yourself, "When I finally get to heaven, I'd like to ask God: 'Why?! Why in the world did You let this happen? Who's responsible for the more than 58,000 names inscribed on the Vietnam War Memorial? Who are the men whose mad acts trigger these global holocausts, God, and what are You planning to do about it?"

Back on July 28, 1914, in Sarajevo, Bosnia – ring any bells? – a Serbian nationalist assassinated Archduke Francis Ferdinand of Austria-Hungary, and his wife. The result? World War I. Four years, three months, and 14 days of pure, unrelenting hell. 32 countries involved. $186 billion in damages – and this in 1918 dollars. A total of 37 million lives lost.

And there may be those among us who would like to spend some quiet time in the library up in heaven, staring into the computer terminals there, and really peer through the divine looking glass and get a sense of what went wrong. Who did this? What price should be paid for those whose lust for power, whose seared consciences, caused so many others to suffer? I've already suggested that even though the true Judgment Scene of the ages happened at Calvary, there are still four separate and distinct phases of divine Judgment that take place here in these last days. So what and when are they?

In his marvelous book, *God Cares, Vol. II*, which is a study on Revelation's prophecies, the late C. Mervyn Maxwell takes us to the book of Daniel for the first Judgment scene. Maybe you've studied the visions of Daniel, the four great beasts that represent the world empires of Babylon, Medo-Persia, Greece, and Rome. Any good history book will validate the uncanny accuracy of what God showed His servant Daniel. Then the key events of the Middle Ages, where pagan Rome evolved into a global Christian power still centered IN Rome. Of course, that historic time line brings us right down into the last century or two. Then, in chapter 7, beginning in verse 9, we find a heavenly scene where Jesus, or, as the Bible puts it, "one like a Son of Man," approaches the Ancient of Days. Verse 10 tells us: "The court was seated, and the books were opened."

I've already suggested that we could call this a kind of "Pre-Advent Judgment." It happens in the last days; the time lines of history, and this event happening after the world empires and after the events of the Middle Ages, bring us down into the modern era. And we have Jesus Christ, up in heaven, coming together with His Father to open the books. And certainly, before the Second Coming of Jesus to this earth, a determination has got to be made about who's saved and who's lost. Over in Daniel 12:1 we find this reference to the Second Coming: "But at that time," after the trouble and distress at the end, "your people – everyone whose name is found written in the book – will be delivered."

So a decision is made. And . . . made public. Who has a relationship with God, and who doesn't? That's Judgment, isn't it? And what a wonderful thing it is to know that Jesus and God are together in wanting you and me to be found in relationship with them! That's fantastic assurance.

But then Jesus comes again. The Bible talks over and over about this guarantee: "Behold, I come quickly! And My reward is with Me!" And Christ Himself, in His parable about the sheep and goats found in Matthew 25, does separate the human race into these two groups. Saved, and Lost. Redeemed, and Unrepentant. I guess that's not really Judgment, but simply a carrying *out* of the Judgment He and His Father already accomplished in the heavenly courts above. Although, for us, it will seem like Judgment happens then.

Well, you would think that the great "Sheep and Goats" metaphor would be the end of it all. But there's a Phase Three, and it's what I've already alluded to. If you go over to Revelation chapter 20, we discover that during what the Bible calls the "millennium," or the thousand years, saved people just like you and me will sit on thrones and judge. "I saw thrones," John the Revelator writes, "on which were seated those who had been given authority to judge."

And here, during these thousand years, is when we can look at the video monitors and finally pin down just what happened, and why, and how. World War One. And Two. Why a plane went down with your loved one on it. Why God allowed your spouse to die of leukemia. What really happened with the JFK assassination and the O. J. Simpson trial? Who is guilty? And HOW guilty? Did God do right when He saved such-and-such person? Or when He DIDN'T save someone you thought would surely have a front-page address in the heavenly Book of Life?

And perhaps we're doing two things, really, during the millennium and this "Phase Three." First of all, we're just satisfying our minds regarding the Judgment decisions that God and Jesus have already made. Now, maybe you won't feel like doing that. On the other hand, maybe you already DO have some questions. And what a quietly comforting and faith-building thing it will be to go through the evidence yourself, at a human pace. Carefully. Thoughtfully. And time after time, your heart is satisfied when you discover that, through all the horrors of this planet's sad history – the wars and rumors of wars, the planes that went down, the people who had so many opportunities to choose Jesus Christ, and never did – you discover that God always did the wisest thing. "I wouldn't change a thing," you finally say as you marvel at His wisdom and love, His second- and third-mile efforts to save the lost. I've already confessed how I like the way Dr. Jack Blanco describes the First Angel's message here in Revelation 14: "Stand in awe of God and give glory to Him, because the time has come for Him to clear HIS name and to judge the world."

But there's one more thing. Because although sentence has been passed on those who have rebelled against God, that sentence hasn't yet been carried out. The destruction of the wicked happens, the Bible says, at the END of the thousand years. You can read it in chapter 20, starting in verse 7. After all is said and done, after Satan's last attempt to overthrow the City, the Bible tells us: "But fire came down from heaven and devoured them."

This is hard truth, and yet good truth, really. Because "devoured" is "devoured." And I believe God is able to completely sweep away all traces of sin and evil at the end. After all, chapter 21 is entitled "The New Jerusalem." But is it possible that some of those who rebelled with the greatest ferocity, or who helped to trigger and mastermind World War I back in 1914 will experience more heartache and more mental anguish – and maybe even more pain – when God's last outpouring of holy fire consumes the rebel armies? And perhaps that is partly what the saints in heaven will participate in deciding during those thousand years. It's interesting that the Apostle Paul, in First Corinthians 6, asks: "Don't you realize that we Christians will judge and reward the very angels in heaven?"

Meaning the rebel angels of Satan, certainly, who are the only ones slated to receive divine punishment.

Well, that's it. The Judgment. Happening in a way that brings you and me into a full and unshakable appreciation for the wisdom of God, and the incredible love of Jesus in saving us.

Let me say this before we move on. The way you've learned these Revelation mysteries might be dramatically different from what you're discovering here. I know that. I've got books here in my office from good and wise Christian students, and my, what a variety of scenarios are there! And these are godly people. We've got to be so humble in our study, and as we pray for each other.

But the bottom line is this: JESUS SAVES! Hold onto that! Hold onto Jesus. Judgment is a wonderfully moot Bible study topic if you're committed to Him, and if you're trusting in Him, and if you're living daily and hourly in the shadow of His saving cross.

11

A DEBATE AT DISNEY WORLD

It's one of the most thought-provoking books to come along in a pretty long time, and it focuses on a Disney World vacation involving a dad and his daughter. In their recent Christian bestseller, *How Now Shall We Live?* – playing off of Francis Schaeffer's book, *How THEN Shall We Live?* – Chuck Colson and Nancy Piercey take 559 pages to describe for readers why the Christian faith is what they call a "worldview." It's not just a way to get away from this sorry old planet, and get yourself up to heaven, although Christianity accomplishes that. But it's also a complete blueprint, a detailed, designed, divinely formulated plan, a strategy, for life and survival down here. Now. As people and as families and as nations.

"Only Christianity," they write in the preface, "offers a way to live in line with the real world. . . . Genuine Christianity is a way of seeing and comprehending all reality. It is a worldview."

It's a deep and scholarly book, as these two gifted believers draw from an incredible array of philosophers, both secular and religious. They explain some of the hard terms we might not know, like *existentialism*, an attitude which they define like this: "Life is absurd, meaningless; . . . the individual self must create his own meaning by his own choices."

Well, instead of Aristotle and Plato, what does this have to do with Donald Duck and Pluto and a vacation to Orlando? Colson's chapter entitled "Creation: Where Did We Come From, and Who Are We?", begins with a father-daughter trip to Disney World. Dave Mulholland is there with his fifteen-year-old to see Epcot Center. Of course, she'd rather go on five thousand roller coasters, but with a sigh she finally gets with Dad into the line for that huge AT&T "Spaceship Earth" globe.

Dave actually has an ulterior motive for the Disney World trip. In recent weeks it's seemed like Katy was struggling spiritually. Not wanting to go to church. Marijuana in her purse. And just a general attitude of antagonism toward the family's core religious values. She appears ready to just chuck it all. And so Dave is hoping for some time to have one-on-one discussions, maybe between rides while they have some cotton candy.

But inside Epcot Center, they sit down in a semicircle theater for a multimedia presentation called "The Living Seas." Maybe you've seen it too. And as they watch this wonderfully put together show, as only the Disney people can, the narrator's voice describes for this 15-year-old high school kid the incredible, odds-defying miracle that kick-starts life. "Deep within the cluster of slowly forming planets," he says, "is a small star of just the right size, a sphere just the right distance from its mother star. Somewhere in the endless reaches of the universe, on the outer edge of the galaxy of a hundred-thousand-million suns." And on this one small world, after billions of years, "tiny, single-celled plants that captured the energy of the sun" produce a spark of oxygen . . . and the first organisms begin to form.

And after the lights come on, and Dave leads his daughter outside where they buy some lunch, the discussion begins. Is there a God out there who created life? Or did these "Living Seas," after endless millennia of pounding up on a lifeless beach, suddenly create their own world?

Well, it's an amazing book, and I certainly invite you to get a copy from Tyndale and read it for yourself: *How Now Shall We Live?*, by Chuck Colson and Nancy Pearcey. But back to this question of Christianity being a "worldview." Because as Dave Mulholland said to his daughter during a rather heated lunch there outside the Norway Exhibit, "But *everything* is at stake here, Katy." If all forms of life, including his own ancestors, just climbed out of the primordial soup on their own and turned from monkeys into men, if existentialism is an accurate description of the way things are on planet earth – "Life is absurd, meaningless, and . . . the individual self must create his own meaning by his own choices" – then everything was lost. His worldview was at an end.

What IS the worldview of the Christian faith? I'm sure different expressions of it have been given by different people; here is how Colson and Pearcey express it. In fact, they suggest that all world-views, not just the Christian one, must address the following: "Every worldview can be analyzed by the way it answers three basic questions: Where did we come from, and who are we (*creation*)? What has gone wrong with the world (*fall*)? And what can we do to fix it (*redemption*)?"

And that's it. One: Where'd we come from? Two: Why are things so bad? And Three: How's it going to get fixed? Any life philosophy worth even the price of a one-day pass to Disney World has got to address those three questions. And even those among us who have given up trying to find an answer to #1 – "Where did we come from?" – are eternally interested in #2. Why are things so bad? Why did Dylan Klebold and Eric Harris shoot their class-mates? Why does God permit Hitler and Slobodan Milosevic to act as they do? Why are there earthquakes? Why did Alaska Airlines flight #261 go down at Point Mugu, right near our Voice of Prophecy radio studios? And question #3: Is there any way out of our mess? Even when the economy's good, can any American president bring us back to moral soundness? Can a rising stock market fix the problems of corporate greed and prostitution and child abuse and Internet porn?

Well, Chuck Colson's 559 pages would not have had to be written if the citizens of this world would simply notice a verse of Scripture exactly 15 words long. Here we are still meditating about this first galactic angel of Revelation 14 and the import of his message. After announcing that we need to fear God and give Him glory, and that judgment is about to commence, the angel adds these 15 vital words: "Worship Him that made heaven, and earth, and the sea, and the fountains of waters."

It's a bit ironic that this verse, Revelation 14:7, addresses the exact same thing as that Epcot Center exhibit: "The Living Seas." But the Word of God tells us – and this is the very heart of what John calls the everlasting gospel – that God Himself made the living seas. He made heaven, and earth, and the sea, and the fountains of waters. "The sea and all its sources," says the *Living Bible* paraphrase. Maybe you noticed just one point, that God is the Creator, and missed the second. But look again: "*Worship* Him that made heaven, and earth, and the sea, and the fountains of waters."

If there's one announcement planet earth needs to hear in this new millennium, it's that we need to worship God again. Not our thriving economy. Not the Information Superhighway which is going to make life so perfect. Not ourselves: our minds, our learning power, our reasoning skills. Not our human achievements: our good grades, our high-paying, high-tech jobs, the Disney Worlds we create, the dot.com companies we start up. The last-day message for planet earth is this: "Worship God again. *Return* to the worship of the God who made it all."

In C. S. Lewis' autobiography, *Surprised By Joy*, he describes how God began to make His final moves to convert this determined atheist. The crucial chapter is entitled "Checkmate," by the way, and the little lead quote is quite interesting. It's by George MacDonald, a writer Lewis greatly admired, and it goes like this: "The one principle of hell is – 'I am my own.'"

In other words, I worship SELF. I made myself; I created my own empire, my own surroundings. There is no God, only the mysterious surge of life forces all around us, the one-in-a-trillion "spark" of life, or a Big Bang, or whatever . . . and I got here all on my own. Just the opposite, in terms of worldview, from what this powerful angel "flying in the midst of heaven" tells us: "Worship

Him who made the heavens and the earth."

As he finishes up his book, C. S. Lewis, now a brand new believer, writes about how he realized finally that God was to be worshiped simply because He WAS God. Simply because He had created the universe. Not so much because God was good – although Lewis soon realized that He was. Not because He sent His Son to die for our sins – although Lewis soon realized that too, becoming one of the world's greatest apologists for the message of Calvary. Not because there was a heaven to get into or a hell to stay out of. But just because God was God, because God had, as it says here, "made heaven, and earth, and the sea, and the fountains of waters." "God was to be obeyed simply because He was God," he wrote. And what a safeguard, what a protection, what a secure worldview we walk into when we first make that discovery!

12

CRYING IN THE CHAPEL

In his book, *The Crisis of the End Time*, my friend Marvin Moore
tells a story that happened to him, oh, about 35 years ago now. He
was attending a Christian youth rally . . . and this had to be about
35 years ago, because he's less of a youth today than I am, and I'm
looking at my fast-approaching 50s. But he has a vivid memory of
that meeting, and of who was leading the singing. It happened to
be our very own John Thurber, who used to be in our Voice of
Prophecy quartet.

Anyway, John asked the congregation to stand and sing with him
the great classic song by John Lowry, "Shall We Gather at the
River." And as Marvin began to sing with all the other believers,
he just got a picture in his head of someday being in heaven,
maybe standing there on the banks of the River of Life. With good
friends there, sharing and talking about how incredible the New
Jerusalem was.

But one more variable kind of injected itself. Because Marvin had
been going through a rather tough time just then. Some personal
trials. And all at once, as he sang with the others, "Shall We
Gather at the River," the desire to be in heaven was just huge.
HUGE! He wanted to be there so bad. And without realizing it,
all of a sudden he was crying. Tears coming down his cheeks.
And a friend of his noticed and came over, and without saying a
word just put an arm around Marvin; somehow they got through
that song together.

Well . . . 35 years. And he still remembers singing that song. And
here's what he writes in his book about that memory: "I needed
that. I needed his hug, and I needed to think about heaven that
morning and weep." And then he adds this very personal testimony: *"That was holy joy."*

It was holy joy, he suggests, because it was *worship*. Him connecting up with God, with the King of the universe – in the proper relationship: Creature . . . and Creator. A man . . . and the Maker of that man. Just Marvin and God: "Shall we gather at the river?"

On the very same page he tells another story on himself, this one more recent. He and his wife were visiting a college church in Lincoln, Nebraska. It was a big, full church, and so they had two services. He and his wife went to the early church service, and enjoyed beyond words the experience of singing and hearing the huge pipe organ. They did an opening hymn that lifted God up for His love and majesty. "I love to sing those hymns," Marvin writes, "because they transport me to the heavenly sanctuary. I get a picture in my mind of God on His throne and millions of the redeemed standing before Him with all the holy angels. I imagine that I'm among them, my arms uplifted, praising God and Jesus Christ."

Well, on this particular Sabbath morning, the same thing happened. That organ was just taking him right up to heaven; the words were so meaningful. And all at once, he couldn't go on. The tears of joy were there, and he couldn't sing. After a line or two, he tried again . . . and just couldn't do it. He was so caught up in worship that he choked up; he had to stop and simply revel in the joy of the Lord, the tears. "I imagined that I was listening to the angels, the 144,000, and the vast multitude from every nation, tribe, and language praising God before His throne." And then those same four words again: "*That was holy joy.*"

That was such a moving worship experience, he confesses, that when it came time for the second service, he said to his wife, "Honey, you go on home to Mom and Dad's place if you want to, but I'm going to stay for the second service." And then his P.S.: "I just had to worship God again."

I guess a lot of us could tell stories like Marvin's. "Amazing

Grace," maybe. Some of us just cannot get through that song. Forget it. Have you heard it done by the bagpipes? It blows me away. I don't know why, but God and worship are just IN that song.

Or "The Hallelujah Chorus." Or "I Bowed on My Knees and Cried Holy." I'm sure you must have a title too – a song title that brings the tears and holy joy.

But let's go back to something Marvin said right in the middle of his story. He imagined being up in heaven, and singing with the angels and with the "144,000." In fact, that's the title of his chapter: "The Spiritual Experience of the 144,000." And maybe you've noticed that mysterious number which comes here in Rev. 14:1, right after the end of chapter 13 and another mysterious number: the dreaded "666" of the Antichrist.

Both of these numbers are outside the scope of our target seven verses in the middle of Revelation chapter 14, and I'm having enough difficulty staying on track without detouring over to these additional mysteries! But consider the topic of worship, and the experience God's people are going to have here in these last days of earth's history.

"Then I saw a Lamb," John writes. That would be Jesus, of course. ". . . Standing on Mount Zion in Jerusalem, and with Him were 144,000 who had His Name and His Father's Name written on their foreheads. And I heard a sound from heaven like the roaring of a great waterfall or the rolling of mighty thunder. It was the singing of a choir accompanied by harps. This tremendous choir – 144,000 strong – sang a wonderful new song in front of the throne of God and before the four Living Beings and the twenty-four Elders; and no one could sing this song except those 144,000 who had been redeemed from the earth. For they are spiritually undefiled, pure as virgins, following the Lamb wherever He goes." (*Living Bible*)

Isn't that an incredible word picture? I have to confess that I don't know all the details about who will make up the 144,000. Christians debate that, probably even more than they do the details about these "Three Angels' Messages." But there are some things we do know about these people.

First of all, they have Jesus' name, and God's name, written on their foreheads. Maybe just figuratively speaking; we don't know. But what a wonderful thought: to be a person who has God's name, and our Redeemer Jesus' name, right there on our foreheads, in our minds. We love to think about the goodness of God; we love to consider all that Jesus has done for us. So the 144,000 will have those kinds of thoughts.

Secondly, we see that these people not only think about Jesus and what He means to them. They follow Him! The original King James puts this on their resumé: "These are they which follow the Lamb whithersoever He goeth."

It seems that obedience to Jesus is at the very heart of the Three Angels' Messages. Loyalty. Faithfulness. And obedience.

But then this third, crucial point. These people, this saved bunch of sinners from the one rebellious, lost world – "redeemed from the earth," it says – love to worship. Mark that down and under-line it a hundred times and then put your Bible and church hymnal next to it. The people of God in the last days will be people who love to worship God. They love to sing. They love to look up at heaven with tears in their eyes and think about God on His throne. They love the words to the new song by Jack Hayford: "Majesty! Worship His majesty!" They love to pray. They love to be in church. They love to arrive, and they hate to leave.

In his book, *The Crisis of the End Time*, after telling his two sto-ries, Marvin makes this biblical observation: "The 144,000 will be above all else a worshiping community!" And then he adds: "I believe that those who proclaim the Three Angels' Messages" – which we're studying right here – "in earth's darkest hour will be a community of people who praise God in glorious, rapturous, joyful worship. And . . . until we learn to really *worship*, we won't really proclaim the message."

What do you think of that? Remembering that this first angel is really US – that we are the ones to proclaim this all-important first message – let's drill ourselves on that message again: "Fear God, and give glory to Him; for the hour of His judgment has come. And *worship* Him who made heaven, and earth, and the sea, and the fountains of waters."

So right here in this last great trilogy of announcements, or warnings, or invitations, is a call to worship. Worship God because He's the Creator. Worship Him because judgment is coming. But most of all, worship Him because you love Him, because the name of His Son – and HIS name too – are written in your forehead, fixed in your mind and sealed in your heart.

13

TOWERS AND TYRANTS

I still remember watching on CNN and our local news when the first headlines began to come in. A dictator named Saddam Hussein had invaded the neighboring country of Kuwait. His Iraqi troops were justified, he said, in the invasion because Kuwait's overproduction of oil was driving down prices and hurting his country. He had an $80 billion deficit from his recent war with Iran, and wanted to spike up the OPEC prices. Plus, he claimed that Iraq had historical claims to Kuwait anyway. Before the rest of the world could blink he had established his own military government in Kuwait City, and "annexed" this tiny neighbor.

And the response? Very quickly, we had Operation Desert Storm, Stormin' Norman Schwarzkopf, F-117 Stealth bombers, "This will not stand!," and all the rest. Maybe you remember this statement by President George Bush: "Just two hours ago Allied air forces began an attack on military targets in Iraq and Kuwait. These attacks continue as I speak. Ground forces are not engaged. This conflict started August second, when the dictator of Iraq invaded a small and helpless neighbor. Kuwait, a member of the Arab League and a member of the United Nations, was crushed, its people brutalized. Five months ago Saddam Hussein started this cruel war against Kuwait. Tonight the battle has been joined."

That brings back memories, doesn't it? And we all rejoiced when this grab for power, this act of naked aggression, ended up failing. We have a reaction against forced submission, against a military strongman demanding allegiance by way of the sword, or by way of the Soviet-made Scud missile.

Here in Revelation 14 we read about a spiritual kingdom called "Babylon." And it's a point of interest that ancient Babylon – you remember King Nebuchadnezzar and fiery furnaces and a Bible hero named Daniel – was located in what is now the country of Iraq. And we might actually find some similarities between the power tactics of Mr. Hussein and the Babylons – both political and spiritual – of Bible times.

It's taken quite a few pages here just to consider the message of this first galactic messenger, who proclaims the "everlasting gospel" and announces that judgment is about to begin. He also invites all of mankind to worship God as the Creator of the universe. That's a crucial point to keep in mind: the Three Angels' Messages are all about *worship*. Worshiping God right, or worshiping some other power in the wrong way.

Now here's verse eight as we move to this second angel. "A second angel followed and said, 'Fallen! Fallen is Babylon the Great, which made all the nations drink the maddening wine of her adulteries'."

So right away we encounter the concept of a dominant power of some kind; notice that it's called "Babylon the Great." It's a fallen power: now, does this mean that it's been defeated – like Hussein eventually was – or that it's *spiritually* fallen? We'll find out, but it's interesting to notice that the Bible describes Babylon as indulging in adultery. Maybe you remember how the King James Version renders it: "She made all nations drink of the wine of the wrath of her fornication."

What do we have here? This is most interesting because, as we've already established, this is a message, a warning, for these last days. Whatever Babylon is, it's a spiritual phenomenon that will happen in these final generations. We studied earlier how the prophecies of both Revelation and Daniel paint a panoramic picture of the great world empires: Babylon (the original), then Medo-Persia, then Greece, then Rome, then the spiritual darkness of the Middle Ages, and then some of these events at the close: this new-and-emerging Revelation 14 Babylon, and the Judgment, etc.

Be aware of one thing immediately. The Babylon here in Revelation 14:8, while it may be a spiritual entity, exerts political might. It throws its weight around among nations. "She made all *nations* drink of the wine of the wrath of her fornication." You almost get a Desert Storm picture of some power emerging which tries to force its neighbors to submit, gobbling up one and then another, and so on.

Let's move momentarily from the book of Revelation, which, of course, is clear at the end of the Bible – Book #66 – and see what kind of pattern emerges in all of God's Word regarding this kingdom called Babylon. Let's recall the link between the ancient empire the Bible hero Daniel, and his three friends, Shadrach, Meshach, and Abednego, were taken to as prisoners, and the old Genesis city known simply as Babel. Babylon – Babel. See the similarity? And it's no accident.

"In Babylonian," writes one commentator, "the name *Bab-ilu* (Babel, or Babylon) meant 'gate of the gods,' but the Hebrews derogatorily associated it with *balal*, a word in their language meaning 'to confuse.'"

You have to time-travel clear back to Genesis chapter 11 to read the story of the first Babylon – or actually, what we know as the Tower of Babel.

"As men moved eastward" – this is after the flood of Noah's generation – "they found a plain in Shinar and settled there." This happens on the very same spot where Nebuchadnezzar's Babylon later came into existence. But not too many generations after the human race should have learned a very wet and watery lesson about being loyal to the God of heaven, people like mighty Nimrod kind of looked up at heaven and shook their fist at the God who lived there.

Notice verse four, which describes the architectural designs of these people, and I'll give a little *pop*! to four words: "Then they said, 'Come, let US build OURSELVES a city, with a tower that reaches to the heavens, so that WE may make a name for OUR-SELVES and not be scattered over the face of the whole earth.'"

So here was an anti-God, self-focused act of rebellion. "Let's trust in self. Let's work to protect self. Let's work to exalt self." In fact, they might well have said: "Hey, let's just flat-out worship self." That's what it boiled down to. The word *Babylon* means: "Gateway to a god." But not the God of heaven, Creator of the universe. No, their god was what these builders saw in the mirror every morning. The NIV text notes pick up on this attitude in their comment: "The people's plans were egotistical and proud." Then they add this: "At Babel rebellious man undertook a united and godless effort to establish for himself, by a titanic human enter-prise, a world renown by which he would dominate God's cre-ation."

So even here in the first pages of the Bible, still in early Genesis, we begin to notice the poisons of Babylon. First of all, self-wor-ship. Or worship of a human system, a human undertaking, a human achievement. Worship directed away from God, and toward man.

Secondly, Babylon reveals a move away from recognizing the authority of God because He's the Creator. Remember how that first Angel in Revelation 14 said: "Worship Him who made the heavens and the earth and the seas and the fountains of waters"? Here in Babel, or this first Babylon, the attitude is 180° away from that. I appreciate the added commentary insight inserted into the *Clear Word* paraphrase by Dr. Jack Blanco: "When [God] saw [the tower], He said, 'This is only the beginning of what these people will attempt to do. They all speak the same language, and if they succeed in this, they'll think that by working together they can do anything they set their minds to. We need to stop them lest they be lifted up with pride *and forget who created them*. Let's confuse their language so that they'll not be able to communicate with each other.'"

Well, you know the story. I guess this is one time where God WAS the Author of confusion! It took Him about two seconds, and all at once people were speaking Swiss and Swahili right next to each other there on the scaffolding. And this sorry little monument to human power and human domination stood deserted in the desert.

What does this mean for us? It's simple, really. If you and I are tempted to think we can save ourselves, then Babylon is beckoning. If we look with pride at our own spiritual growth, and think we can qualify for heaven through our own goodness . . . that's Babylon. If we begin to edge toward the concept that man got here by himself, and that the Creation Story belongs on the same shelf with Santa Claus and the Tooth Fairy, then we've begun to dwell in a 21st century tower of Babylon. That's the warning and the invitation here: "Worship GOD . . . who made the heavens, and the earth, and the universe, and each one of us. Worship the God who keeps your heart beating in your chest as you read these words."

14

WORSHIPING AT WACO

Her story is found just in a book appendix, and it's some of the toughest reading I've ever done. Diana Ishikawa – and that's not her real name – was a disciple of the late David Koresh in the ill-fated Waco compound. Just weeks after the Branch Davidian empire went up in flames, she agreed to be interviewed by Christian writer Richard Abanes, co-author of a book entitled *Prophets of the Apocalypse*.

I thank God she's alive today, but several things hurt almost beyond description. First, she became one of the many "wives" of this cult leader. Diana was Number Six, and the first girl to become pregnant by Koresh. As he spun his mad theologies about the daughters of Moab and the "Bride of Christ," and how he alone should possess all the women in his flock, this 20-year-old girl finally agreed to give herself to him. Most of his other "wives" were much younger; in fact, in a rare moment of humor she admits: "I was the old lady of the bunch."

The thing that hurts on a rather personal level – and of course, we all mourn the loss of the 86 cult victims – is that this young girl, Diana Ishikawa, was seduced into the Davidian nightmare right out of my own Adventist church family. David and Debbie Bunds: also former Seventh-day Adventists. Mark Brault, an Adventist. Many sincere Christian people, men and women who loved to read their Bibles and pray, went down this dark and fatal road.

Knowing this, it makes it difficult to pick up a Bible these days and return to the very book of the Bible that seemed to cause such confusion to these religious devotees. Because David Koresh did a lot of reading from the book of Revelation. He expounded doctrine to his Waco flock from its 22 chapters. He was a King James Version-only kind of teacher. David Bunds told these same interviewers later: "He delivered [doctrine] well. He's charismatic. He speaks with authority. He talks like he really knows what he's talking about. He can quote the Bible profusely. He will barrage you. He's probably ten times better than the most elite Jehovah's Witness. . . . He can quote entire chapters, especially from the Old Testament prophecies. He'll quote entire chapters of Isaiah just right off the top of his head. He'll barrage you and just overwhelm you."

The present-tense references in this segment help us realize that the interview happened while the Waco standoff was still going on. But here is a group of people who were devoutly religious. In a sense, they were doing what these three Angels in Revelation chapter 14 are talking about: they were worshiping. They were thick into worship in a way that you and I have probably never experienced. Worship was a 24-hour-a-day, no-holds-barred commitment for David Koresh and his followers.

What does this all mean? Well, we look back to that April 19, 1993 fire, and realize that there's such a thing as true worship, and there's such a thing as false worship. IT IS NOT ENOUGH TO WORSHIP! And even these precious people, these well-meaning, devoted Bible students, fell into a blinding and fatal trap of worshiping WRONG.

It's risky to look again at the message of Angel #2, and realize that in the sweaty, marathon nighttime study sessions in Waco, Texas, David Koresh probably read this same verse. But let's trust in God to protect us as WE study His sure Word. Here's that message, found in verse 8: "Fallen! Fallen is Babylon the Great, which made all the nations drink the maddening wine of her adulteries."

Of course we can look back now and realize that Waco itself is a fallen legacy of ashes and death. But I'm sure that Koresh told his followers that Babylon was what they had come out OF, that the Adventist Church and the other Christian churches where he'd recruited them were Babylon. And thank God, he, David Koresh, a.k.a. Vernon Howell, a.k.a. "The Lamb of Revelation" had come along just in time to rescue them.

It's not my purpose here to try to defend my church or your church, or to attack the Branch Davidian saga as being Babylon or NOT-Babylon. Obviously, none of us would ever think WE were dwelling in Babylon. We're sure we're all right, that our faith movement is part of the New Jerusalem. But what a sobering thing it is, for all of us, across the board, to read these three invitations to worship God, the Creator of heaven and earth. And to also read a warning, a get-out-now! alarm against staying in a system that is devotedly worshiping . . . but worshiping WRONG.

In *The Knowledge of the Holy*, by A. W. Tozer, he says this in the preface: "It is impossible to keep our moral practices sound and our inward attitudes right while our idea of God is erroneous or inadequate. If we would bring back spiritual power to our lives, we must begin to think of God more nearly as He is."

That's an incredible thought, isn't it? If we have wrong concepts of God, our worship will be wrong. Never forget that in the Old Testament, Babylon was a worshiping place. They DID worship. Daniel three tells the unforgettable story about the great image Nebuchadnezzar set up on the Plain of Dura. And very next thing, he wanted to force the entire kingdom to bow down and worship that image. It's a crucial Babylon story, with huge implications for those of us who read Revelation here in the 21st century. But when the Word of God tells us that Babylon is a fallen power, it's referring to the fact that false worship is involved. Bowing down is involved . . . but to the wrong authority.

Chapter One of Dr. Tozer's book bears this title: "Why We Must Think Rightly About God." "What comes into our minds when we think about God is the most important thing about us. The history of mankind will probably show that no people has ever risen above its religion, and man's spiritual history will positively demonstrate that no religion has ever been greater than its idea of God."

So what is our protection today? I could tell you here to simply listen to me: that I would define God for you, that I would tell you what Babylon is, and how to get out of it. "Stick with me," I could say . . . and that would be the exact same formula for death-by-fire that David Koresh used.

Part of our protection is found just one verse earlier, in the message from the first Angel. "Worship God," the Angel says. "Fear God. Worship the Creator. Give glory to the Creator." The great mistake at Waco was when devotion shifted away from God, and came to be directed toward a human being. In Babylon, the object of worship was that great golden image standing 90 feet high; actually, Nebuchadnezzar was seeking worship for *himself*, and using the image just as a symbol to direct the worship of the masses toward him. For David Koresh, the same goal: worship of self instead of God. He was the Seventh Angel, the Living Prophet of God, the Lamb of God, the re-embodying of Christ. And he accepted worship, both sexual and spiritual.

This is the challenge we face: to keep worship focused and centered on GOD.

Just as I was writing this very chapter for radio back in early 2000, my secretary brought in the mail and put it on my desk. With a letter from Thomas Nelson Publishers: *E-Quake!*, the envelope teaser announced. "Unlocking the Book of Revelation," by Pastor Jack Hayford. Brand new videos that explore the same messages we've been cautiously digging into here.

Now, is that safe? Does Pastor Hayford know what Babylon is, and what true worship is versus false? He's just a mere man, and I'm a lot more "mere" than he is, believe me. How safe can we be in our study?

Well, we all have the same security system as we study: a relentless focus on the worship of GOD. God the Creator of heaven and earth. And the worship of Jesus Christ, who is the proper, and the only, subject of the book of Revelation. In fact, Pastor Hayford's letter has an explicit commitment regarding "the author's faithfulness in drawing the listener back to the true focal point of the study – Jesus."

Are you worried here in these last days that you, too, might be led astray, that there's a Waco tombstone out there with your name on it? Do you get afraid sometimes that, in all the confusion of religious theories about Revelation, you might end up marching INTO Babylon instead of out of it? If your focus is on Jesus Christ, and if your commitment in worship is to fall on your knees before God the Creator, then YOU DO NOT NEED TO HAVE THAT FEAR! Take comfort from the wonderful Good News, the saving news, that comes for all of us at the conclusion of the *Third* Angel's Message: "This calls for patient endurance on the part of the saints who obey God's commandments and remain faithful to Jesus."

And that's it. Obedience to God the Creator. And remaining faithful to Jesus. That's true worship. And that's everlasting security.

15

BRIDGES TO BABYLON

There was a lively discussion when the document first began to rumble around on the Internet back in May of 1998. The official title was as follows: "Apostolic Letter Dies Domini of the Holy Father John Paul II to the Bishops, Clergy and Faithful of the Catholic Church on Keeping the Lord's Day Holy." And for something like 40 pages, and 87 sections, the leader makes an impassioned plea for his flock, "My esteemed Brothers in the Episcopate and the Priesthood, Dear Brothers and Sisters!," to begin keeping Sunday again. Jay McNally, the executive director of a Detroit group, Call to Holiness, told reporters: "This appears to be the strongest words the pope has issued. Period."

You can imagine that in my own faith community, the Adventist Church – which has studied and proclaimed the importance of the Sabbath since our inception back in the mid-1800s – this was an incredible turn of events. And really, out of 87 points made by Pope John Paul II, good Seventh-day Adventist Christians were nodding their heads on a great many of his assertions. One of our top theologians, who has written about the eternal nature of the Sabbath for years, and who had done a doctoral dissertation on that very subject, wrote: "The Pope's reflections on the theological meaning of the Sabbath are most perceptive, and should thrill especially Sabbatarians."

However, there's a red flag which did go off as we all read the document. In Section 64, the pope writes eloquently about how faithful Catholics through the centuries have faced the challenge of trying to keep Sunday when the state didn't give them that 24-hour period off. In the fourth century, he points out, "Civil law of the Roman Empire [recognized] the weekly occurrence, determining that on 'the day of the sun' the judges, the people of the cities and the various trade corporations would not work." But since that time, there have been many periods in history where the governmental power did NOT give all workers Sunday as a full-fledged day of rest. And of course, here in the 21st century the entire world has gone to the mall, so to speak, seven days a week. Dust-covered Blue Laws are something we in the United States are almost embarrassed about.

Then in Section 66, the pope describes how the Church, in making her own laws, has tried to help the common man in his struggle to keep Sunday holy. But notice this, at the end of that section: "In this matter, my predecessor Pope Leo XIII in his encyclical Rerum Novarum spoke of Sunday rest as a worker's right *which the state must guarantee*."

In other words, the Church has a right to look to Washington, D.C., and to Number Ten Downing Street, and to the Kremlin, and to the other governments of the world and say: "YOU'VE got to help us be good Christians. You must make Sunday a holiday for everyone – close the shops, lock up the factories, shut down the football stadiums – so that believers can truly enter into Sabbath rest."

Then in Section 67, which follows immediately after, we find this challenge: "Therefore, also in the particular circumstances of our own time, Christians will naturally strive to ensure that civil legislation respects their duty to keep Sunday holy."

Right there, the cheering for this document dies down a little bit. Let me tell you why.

And as I do so, let me stay away from the obvious objection that arises in this high-tech era from our pluralistic nation. I'm a Seventh-day Adventist. Should the government also shut down all the stores and ballparks on Saturday, and remove all temptation, so that people in my church family will find it easier to obey God? What about all of our Moslem neighbors – and Southern California has several million of them? Should Friday become a third day of rest, with our Senate and House "helping" all of us by closing the restaurants and gas stations on that day too? You see the point. But really, that's the tip of the iceberg regarding the concern we should all feel. There is a sense – and I say this carefully, looking into my own heart too – where anytime we look to the state to aid, or assist, or legislate, or require our worship . . . we have entered into what the book of Revelation describes as "Babylon."

Here in chapter 14 there is a mysterious fallen kingdom the second Angel announces AS Babylon. "Fallen! Fallen is Babylon the Great, which made all the nations of the earth drink the maddening wine of her adulteries."

It's very easy to look around and point a finger at some other group and give them a condemning label. I don't want to do that. But let's backtrack to the original Babylon of Daniel chapter three. There we find the unforgettable story of how Shadrach, Meshach, and Abednego refused to bow down to the golden image King Nebuchadnezzar had set up on the Plain of Dura. And we notice that the story isn't just about worship, but especially about *enforced* worship. Worship where the State stepped in and told people, "You WILL bow down. We will help you bow down, and the motivation to help you is this fiery furnace over here."

It's a fundamental reality that Babylon involves false worship. But it can also involve worship that otherwise would be good . . . IF the element of coercion, of force, is introduced. And the Word of God tells us prophetically that in these last days, there will indeed be a rising up of a Babylon power. A power that seeks to enforce worship through the power of the governments of the world.

Shall we consider clues? Right here in this very verse of Scripture, Revelation 14:8, we hear the marching of boots. "Fallen is Babylon the Great, which *made* all the nations drink the maddening wine of her adulteries."

Here is a religious power, this Babylon. But this Babylon phenomenon is actually able to require governments of the world to do her
bidding. In fact, I've read suggestions by theologians that the
word, "adulteries," or "fornication," as the King James puts it,
might well refer to the fact that this church entity reaches out TO
the government to enforce her will. That would be fornication,
wouldn't it, an unholy alliance between church and state. There
are those today, especially every election year, who decry the
famous First Amendment wall of separation. I want to tell you – I
don't. That wall is our great protection. That wall is what keeps
us out of Babylon.

As we return to Revelation 13 we find more traces of "Babylon"
here too. The described beast power makes war on God's saints,
we read. In verse eight: "All inhabitants of the earth will *worship*
the beast – all whose names have not been written in the book of
life."

Then in verse 15, this chilling announcement: "He was given
power to give breath to the image of the first beast, so that it could
speak and cause all who refused to worship the image to be
killed."

And then right here is where the Bible tells about the dreaded
"mark of the beast," and the number 666, etc. Which, I fully confess, is a mysterious arena which continues to baffle the best Bible
students in the world. If I gave you my own interpretations, I
might be many miles off the track.

All I CAN humbly propose is the broad principle here. The threat
of Babylon has always existed where good people tried to make
other people good too. It happened to Daniel's three friends.
"Bow down and pray or we'll burn you up." In a 1999 *U.S. News
& World Report* article, Jeffery Sheler quotes from New Testament
scholar N. T. Wright about a violent faction known as the
Shammaite Pharisees: "While for modern Christians, zeal is

'something you do on your knees, or in evangelism, or in works of charity, for the first-century Shammaites, "zeal" was something you did with a knife.'"

The same thing happened in the Dark Ages. Maybe you happened to read, not too many months ago, a great cover article in *Newsweek* by Kenneth Woodward entitled "2000 Years of Jesus: Holy Wars to Helping Hands – How Christianity Shaped the World." And he takes us through the long list of horrors where religious people took hold of the sword of force. "The legacy of medieval 'Christendom' had its darker side," he writes: "Acting on the premise that error has no rights, the church created the Inquisition. . . . a monument to religious intolerance and a reminder of what can happen when church and state share total authority."

Well, Christians can and do repent of past tragedies. And we thank God for that. But when the Bible prophetically tells us about the future rise of the spirit of Babylon again, all of us should be vigilant in wanting to protect the flame of liberty, freedom of conscience, that should burn in the heart of every person.

And God's invitation to you is this: hold onto this principle of freely offered worship to God the Creator. That's what this is all about. God invites us, "Worship Me. But worship Me FREELY!" Coerced worship where the governments of the world "help" us keep the Sabbath, "help" make us holy . . . that kind of worship is unacceptable to God. It always has been, and it always will be.

The words, "Come unto Me," are never a threat – but always an invitation.

16

"IS THAT YOUR FINAL ANSWER?"

They're the hottest thing around, not just in Christian fiction, but in general fiction. Authors Tim LaHaye and Jerry Jenkins have hit the mother lode with their series, "Left Behind." The apocalyptic adventures of Buck Williams and Rayford Steele in *Assassins*, number six in the lineup, debuted in August of 1999 at #2 on the New York Times best-seller list, which doesn't even count the Christian bookstores. Number five, *Apollyon*, came in at #1 on Amazon.com. "That's Grisham/Clancy territory," said *Entertainment Weekly*, in a gushing two-part series on how Christian projects are invading the secular world.

Back in November of '99, *Newsweek's* religion writer, Kenneth Woodward, had a cover story called "The Way the World Ends." The Y2K deadline was just about nine weeks away back then, so people were percolating with great interest about millennial happenings, secret raptures, etc. He pointed his readers to surveys which show that a whopping 40% of Americans do believe that this old world is going to come to an end according to Revelation scenarios, in some type of "Battle of Armageddon."

Hal Lindsey's apocalyptic bestseller, *The Late Great Planet Earth*, he also pointed out, had sold something like 28 million copies since it came out in the 1970s.

Of course, skeptics and scholars alike are quick to counter that many, many of the predictions in Mr. Lindsey's book have already failed over the years. A great number of the doomsday predictions sincere Christians have made never came to fruition. In fact, according to the research done by Kenneth Woodward for this story, many contemporary Christian theologians figure that all these things John the Revelator wrote about actually happened – in some interpretation or another – during the trials of the first-century

Christian church. "John was not predicting a distant future," he writes.

And as we continue to study the prophecies of Revelation, particularly here in chapter 14, we face a distinct challenge. In a way, it's like the old children's game of "Blind Man's Buff." Does that ancient game ring a bell? You have a blindfold on, and now you've got to try to grope in the darkness for someone or something to hang onto. How can you know where your friends are? Or where all the bumps in the road might be, the potholes and land mines?

It's like that here, isn't it? The book of Revelation warns us with fearsome language about a spiritual organization called "Babylon." But what is it? WHO is it? Is it here now? Is it coming up later? If "Babylon" happened back in the first century A.D., then can we get on with life?

It says here in chapter 14, in the message of the "Second Angel," that "Babylon is fallen." If that's the case, we don't want to be IN Babylon. In fact, you can go over just four chapters, to Revelation 18, and read a parallel warning there: "Fallen! Fallen is Babylon the Great! She has become a home for demons and a haunt for every evil spirit, a haunt for every unclean and detestable bird." And then this, which is almost word-for-word what we've already read: "For all the nations have drunk the maddening wine of her adulteries. The kings of the earth committed adultery with her."

And again we ask: "But what IS Babylon? This spiritual force isn't listed in the Yellow Pages under that name." I'm not making light of our dilemma. Millions of Christians are vitally interested in these symbols and their interpretations. *Newsweek* Magazine, for this cover article, commissioned the Princeton Survey Research Associates to run a statistical survey, and they found out that 19% of Americans in general – and almost FIFTY percent of people who believe in Bible prophecy – believe that the Antichrist, whatever or whoever that is, is living on this earth right now. Maybe he's named Nicolae Carpathia – that's the assigned name in LaHaye's fictional tale – and maybe not, but if he's walking around in your town or mine right now, that would be a good thing to know.

So here's where we are. We're studying about Babylon . . . but what is it? The Bible warns about an antichrist power . . . but who is HE? Or she? We're supposed to be careful that we don't get the Mark of the Beast – in the forehead or in the hand, it says in Revelation 14:9 – but what IS that Mark? Bar codes? The World Wide Web? How can we avoid it if we don't know what it is? We should watch out for a beast power that has the mysterious number: 666. All right . . . but what does THAT mean? You talk about "Blind Man's Buff"!

And the spiritual ante climbs even one step higher as we sense how these mysterious Bible symbols invade our own lives. If the book of Daniel describes four beasts, and they represent four long-defunct world empires – ancient Babylon, Medo-Persia, Greece, and Rome – that's sterile and safe. But here in Revelation, the angel of God cries out in OUR direction: "Fear God! Give glory to Him!" And then the third Angel: "Don't worship the beast. Don't worship the image of this Babylon beast . . . or you'll feel the wrath of God."

Over in chapter 18 is a verse that comes right in my direction and in yours. After telling us that Babylon the Great has fallen, fallen, we hear a great voice from heaven, and it says this: "Come OUT of her, My people, so that you will not share in her sins, so that you will not receive any of her plagues, for her sins are piled up to heaven, and God has remembered her crimes."

And maybe as you fumble with the blindfold that's wrapped so tightly, blocking your vision, you want to cry out: "God, what are You talking about? What is Babylon? I can't come out if I don't know if I'm IN! I can't come out if I don't know what to come out

OF."

Well, let me share some good news, some words of encouragement as we keep on studying. Obviously, here at The Voice of Prophecy, we think it IS worthwhile to study these ancient Bible prophecies, or we wouldn't expend four radio weeks out of our schedule on the subject. We believe these warnings and promises ARE valid for the 21st century, not just the first century, or we'd have moved on by now. We think Babylon is a last-day entity, not just an ancient empire where Daniel and his three friends hung out.

But I want to tell you something else, and it's this: *We don't need to worry*. Because the book of Revelation is a book offering us "The Revelation of Jesus Christ." Those are the first five words of this book; did you know that? And what that means is this: no matter how these prophecies play themselves out, no matter how their fulfillments come to pass, and in what generation, those who have Jesus Christ as their Savior are in perfect safety. Friend, I believe that with all of my heart. In the very thick of chapter 13, which is about as scary as you can get, with death decrees and 1260 years of persecution for God's people, it then says quietly in verse 10: "This calls for patient endurance and faithfulness on the part of the saints."

Don't you like that? "Patient endurance." Here in chapter 14, which is equally thunderous in its warnings, the same thing again: "This calls for patient endurance on the part of the saints who obey God's commandments and remain faithful to Jesus."

Our friend Daniel, along with Shadrach, Meshach, and Abednego, lived in the first Babylon. It was a place of corruption. It was fallen. It promoted false worship. It tried to coerce worship and had its own death decree. But Daniel and his friends stayed close to God, and they were all right. Here in the end-time, with the return of Babylon – spiritual Babylon this time – we're going to see those same things. Babylon will want our worship. You can read that in chapter 13. It will be a fallen spiritual power. It will try to coerce worship, to demand religious obedience. Right down the line, Babylon #2 will follow the lead of Babylon #1. But those who remain in the hand of God will be safe. Those who follow the Lamb "whithersoever He goeth," will someday stand on the Sea of Glass.

And here's one more thing before we leave the beasts and the brimstone. God isn't going to calculate your salvation, your destiny, on the basis of prophetic correctness. Revelation isn't a puzzle where only the lucky few with the best slide rules are going to get into heaven. We get a picture sometimes of that hard, hard final question, #15, on *Who Wants to Be a Millionaire*? You've already used up your lifelines; you've polled the audience, wasted your 50-50, and burned up your "Phone a Friend." And now Regis Philbin leans in: "Is that your final answer? Your life depends on guessing right, young man. Final answer?" Listen, if you and I are saved in God's kingdom it will be because Jesus died for us on the Cross of Calvary, and because we accepted His death for us on the Cross of Calvary. Not because we outsmarted Kenneth Woodward and Tim LaHaye and guessed right about 666.

It's all right to study "666" and the fallen kingdom of Babylon and the Three Angels' Messages here in Revelation. We've still got a ways to go here in chapter 14. But all the way through, ALWAYS, keep a marker back at John 3:16.

17

AMERICA'S LAST PRESIDENT REVEALED

It caused a bit of a ruckus when the rumor started in my denomination. One of our faithful Adventist pioneers, it was alleged, had received a prophetic message from God. And in the message, this particular person had been told, flat-out, the name of the person who would be President of the United States at the time in history when Jesus Christ returned to earth.

Now, this was decades ago, and especially in an election year I would hasten to inform anyone tuning in that the entire rumor was exactly that: a false rumor! There wasn't a word of truth to it. But as we human beings struggle mightily to slog through these difficult, intricate Bible passages found in the book of Revelation, we might sometimes wish that God would simply sweep aside the smoke and the mirrors and tell us: "Here it is. I'm coming on such-and-such date. So-and-So will be President. All My faithful followers should wait for Me at the base of X Mountain, and I'll be there at the stroke of midnight." Would it be good if God were to communicate with such clarity?

In his standout book, *Disappointment With God*, Philip Yancey echoes the frustration some of us feel as we grapple with these dark mysteries: the beasts and the metaphors. Why doesn't God just show up? we wonder. Why is He so hidden? Why doesn't He seem to answer our prayers? Why can't it be like in the days of Israel, where God was right there with them in that cloud? There wasn't any mystery when God spoke from Mount Sinai. Every person within 50 miles heard Him, and God didn't stutter on a single syllable.

But Yancey goes on to ask: Did the presence of God among them make Israel more mature? Did they grow into abiding faith, a deeper relationship? Or did they stay childlike and vacillating, blown this way and that by every temptation that came along, even with God right there in the camp? Did God perhaps want people who would become seasoned and faithful through adversity, like Job, who would trust Him even in His absence? Does He want people who look for His coming ALL the time, and not just when the predicted President Jones takes the oath of office?

And maybe we could ask the same here. Revelation is a hard book, with baffling interpretations. People disagree on what the beasts and dragons mean. Why doesn't God just say: "Here I come, on such-and-such date. Sometime before that date . . . please get ready"? Well, you know and I know that most of the world would pick up a Bible and get on their knees about three minutes before the announced arrival. Are those the kinds of eternal friendships God wants to have with us? Does He want people who simply want a free ride to a mansion in heaven, or people who will trust Him as a good God even in the darkness, even when some parts of His Word to us remain mysterious?

The skilled Christian author, Pastor F. D. Nichol, who answered the scurrilous rumor about someone knowing the name of the President when Jesus returns to earth, had this to say: "We need to be careful lest our pious desire to learn more fully God's purposes for this world be displaced by an idle curiosity to discover what God has not seen fit to reveal."

And the fact of the matter is this: God hasn't told us when His Son is returning. In fact, Jesus Himself was very explicit that this was something we *weren't* going to be told. "No one knows the day or the hour," He calmly told His followers, and that was 2000 years ago.

I find this to be helpful whenever I read passages in my Bible where all the answers aren't evident. And that's especially true here in Revelation. Have I successfully assigned meanings to every metaphor? Do I know what every beast and every seal and every trumpet stands for? No, I don't. Even when I have opinions, I share them with reluctance, because I'm a very human person, and all humans are fallible. What seems obvious to me might not be obvious to someone else, and it might appear absolutely ludicrous to God, who alone knows what He's planning to do. But that doesn't keep me from studying. That doesn't cause me to stop my spiritual digging at the end of Jude verse 25. Again, the book of Revelation is supposed to be exactly that: a revelation. A revelation of Jesus Christ. So I accept what I do understand, I patiently wait on the rest, and I hang onto the hand of the Revealed One, Jesus Christ, every step of the way.

With that in mind, let's move now to the message of the third and final Angel. We've seen that this chapter 14 is a call to worship. It's an announcement about Judgment. It's a warning that Babylon has fallen. And now the first two Angels are followed by this third One, who begins his proclamation in verse 9: "If anyone worships the beast and his image and receives his mark on the forehead or on the hand, he, too [along with fallen Babylon] will drink of the wine of God's fury, which has been poured out full strength into the cup of His wrath."

Right here we could make a pretty substantial list of the things we don't know for sure! Who is the beast? What about this "image"? And what about this mark, in the forehead or in the hand? The Word of God doesn't tell us exactly what these three things are. And if a person says he or she knows, then they're providing an *interpretation* of prophecy. Which . . . might well be right. I know some incredible Bible students and seminary theologians, and I have great respect for their skills of interpretation. Especially as I realize that some of them are humble, committed Christians who submit their own minds to the leading of the Holy Spirit.

But we always should focus most on what the Bible clearly DOES tell us. What message has God NOT hidden?

First of all, it's not a great leap of logic to say that we do not want to be found in the circumstances described in Revelation 14:9. Whatever the Beast power in Revelation is, we don't want to be found worshiping it!

Remember our initial observation, back at the beginning, that Revelation 14 is all about worship. Go back just to the message of this first Angel, which is found in verse seven. And what do we find? A divine invitation to worship. "Fear God and give Him glory, because the hour of His judgment has come. Worship Him who made the heavens, the earth, the sea and the springs of water."

Frankly, I'm not too overly concerned about identifying this "beast" of the third Angel's message. Why? Because all I have to do is to focus all of MY worship, 110% of it, 24 hours a day, seven days a week on the God of heaven. I make sure I'm not worshiping the beast – any beast – by determining that I'll only worship God.

And I find a second not-mysterious invitation here as well. You and I want to focus like a laser, not just on worshiping the God of heaven, but worshiping Him with a renewed emphasis on His role as our Creator. Notice again: "Worship Him who made the heavens, the earth, the sea and the springs of waters."

I want to make sure that in my daily personal devotions, I kneel before God as my Creator. I want to make sure that in the books I read and the television programs I watch and the CDs I play in my car, God doesn't lose His role as my Creator. I want to make sure that in the church services I attend, there's not one element detracting from God as my Creator . . . whether it's from the Sabbath sermon, the hymns, the theology, the mission work, the prayers, the Bible study curriculum, anything. Because I read here in chapter 14 that I can be protected from falling under the influence of this beast power by remembering always that God is my Creator.

And again I say, this is what we can KNOW. The things we don't know . . .we don't know. But we DO know that in these last days, the central issue is this: Worshiping God *as our Creator*.

I confess – and this is very personal – that right here is one key reason why I chose the Adventist fellowship for my own spiritual home. Because in the heart of the Fourth Commandment, the Sabbath commandment, is the eternal reminder: "Remember the Sabbath day by keeping it holy. Six days you shall labor and do all your work, but the seventh day is a Sabbath to the Lord your God. . . . For in six days *the Lord made* the heavens and the earth, the sea, and all that is in them, but He rested on the seventh day. Therefore the Lord blessed the Sabbath day and made it holy."

And there you have it. So many things in the Bible we don't know, but right here in Exodus 20, I've found a wonderful way, a weekly way, a glorious full 24-hour way to always be reminded that I don't worship the beast, I worship the God of heaven who made this world in six days and rested on the seventh.

If you want last-day protection, you can't do much better than that.

18

WATERGATE CODES

The clues were hiding, silently lurking, on tapes in the basement of the big white house at 1600 Pennsylvania Avenue. They showed obstruction of justice. A coverup. Crimes by the President of the United States. And back in 1974, the puzzle pieces suddenly came out into the open.

I don't know why, but the date August 9 seems to always trigger in my mind the sad conclusion to the Watergate scandal. We've had others since then, certainly. But somehow, every time August 9 comes around, I remember Richard Nixon making his final speech to the staff of the White House. Everybody crying. Then that long walk on the red carpet out to the helicopter which would carry the 37th President to California and private life.

Of course, all of us remember the speech from the Oval Office the night before. "I have never been a quitter. To leave office before my term is completed is abhorrent to every instinct in my body. But as President I must put the interests of America first. America needs a full-time President, and a full-time Congress, particularly at this time with problems we face at home and abroad. To continue to fight through the months ahead for my personal vindication would almost totally absorb the time and attention of both the President and the Congress during a period when our entire focus should be on the great issues of peace abroad and prosperity without inflation at home. Therefore I shall resign the Presidency effective at noon tomorrow."

Well, it was a sad moment. But let's turn our attention to the hidden clues that just sat there on those spools of reel-to-reel tape. The June 23, 1972 conversation between Nixon and Haldeman which spelled certain disaster. It was all there, just waiting for someone to come along and find out the truth.

Here in our study of the book of Revelation, we've pretty much stayed away from a "sort out the clues" philosophy. Good Christians everywhere disagree about what these ancient dreams mean, what the images and beasts and numbers are all about. At the same time, when one of God's mighty Angels warns us that Babylon is fallen, and that we should get out, and that those who worship "the Beast" will share in its eventual fate, its doom, we DO want to know whatever God does see fit to reveal to us. Don't you agree? And we praise God for the plain things He does share: that worshiping the God of heaven as our Creator is a safe protection against dragons and beasts – whatever they represent.

So for a moment, let's carefully adopt a bit of Woodward and Bernstein role: looking for the clues. What does the Bible say about this enemy of heaven, the Beast? Besides the fact that it's going to taste the full measure of God's holy anger in the end?

You really have to go back to chapter 13 to pick up on any details about the beast power. My NIV Bible, by the way, as it describes what Revelation personifies as "Babylon," makes this point in its text notes: "Ancient Babylon in Mesopotamia was the political, commercial and religious center of a world empire. It was noted for its luxury and moral decadence. The title 'Babylon the Great' is taken from Daniel 4:30. According to some, it is used in Revelation for Rome as the center of opposition to God and His people."

Well, that's interpretation. But I think there's truth here. In Daniel's day, Babylon was Nebuchadnezzar's anti-God kingdom. He was its center; he sought glory for himself. He was willing to coerce worship, to demand it. He tried to pull Daniel and his friends away from worshiping God, and force their worship of him. So this description in the NIV is accurate: "The center of opposition to God and His people."

All right. Here in chapter 13, we find that the Dragon – that very clearly is Satan – gives this beast its power. And a throne. And great authority. One of its heads seems to have a fatal wound, and then is miraculously healed. Verse three: "The whole world was astonished and followed the beast." "The world *wondered* after the beast," says the King James.

As we continue into verse five, we find that this religious power, this anti-God entity, blasphemes God. Just like in original Babylon, where Nebuchadnezzar claimed, by force, worship that only God should receive. Here it happens again. No wonder this beast is a kind of Babylon Part Two!

Then an interesting number. The beast "exercises authority," the Bible says, for 42 months. It blasphemes God, slanders the saints, and actually makes war against God's people for 42 months. By the time we get to verse eight, we find that this beast power is being worshiped on a global level, except for those who belong to the Lamb.

Now let's go back just one chapter earlier, to Revelation 12. Here's the dragon mentioned as well: remember, that is a clear reference to the devil. A woman – generally symbolizing a church in prophetic literature – is about to give birth to a Son. The dragon is poised to devour it as soon as it's born. But, verse five, "her child was snatched up to God and to His throne." My NIV text notes say: "[This is] the ascension of Christ."

Which makes sense. The baby Jesus, and the boy Jesus, and the Messiah Jesus, were always the prime targets of Lucifer's rage. The New Testament makes that abundantly plain. But now notice this in verse six: "The woman [that's the pure Church, remember] fled into the desert to a place prepared for her by God, where she might be taken care of for 1,260 days."

A great many Bible students, and I tend to see it their way on this point, subscribe to a interpretation that a day – here it says 1,260 days – represents a year. Which would make this 1,260 years. We can leave that issue to the side for now, but a bit of interesting math comes to our minds. Earlier we find that this beast power persecutes God's people for 42 months. How many days in a month? Thirty. Thirty times 42 is exactly 1,260. Following the resurrection of Jesus, the woman, the church, hides in the desert while the beast power tries to persecute her for 1,260 days. Or years, if you accept that day-year interpretation. So there's a perfect match regarding this beast power's reign of terror against those who are trying to worship God.

But just one more number, if you will. Go with me clear back to the Old Testament, to the ancient book of Daniel. Also a prophetic book. Also filled with mysterious beasts and vivid metaphors. Written, by the way, hundreds of years before John the Revelator, the disciple of Jesus, penned the visions of Revelation on the island of Patmos. Two books, two authors, who never met or knew each other. But here in chapter seven of Daniel, lurking in the presidential tapes and transcripts of the first Babylon, we find the original smoking gun. (To borrow that Woodward/Bernstein metaphor.) Here is a dreadful fourth beast in Daniel's dream, representing pagan Rome. Iron teeth. Bronze claws. Ten horns. And lo and behold, a new horn comes up, uprooting three of the other horns. And this 11th horn has eyes and a mouth. The mouth blasphemes – just like the beast in Revelation 13. It wages war against the saints – just like the beast in Revelation 13. It "oppresses the saints," verse 25 says. One more clue: It will try to change, or think to change, the King James says, "times and laws." Not only does this power, this little horn, try to persecute God's people, and subvert their worship of Him, but it actually tries to change the Law of God. It tampers with His commandments.

And now this intriguing expression: "The saints will be handed over to him for a time, times, and half a time."

In the King James, it's "time, times, and the dividing of time."

What's it mean? Again, we take to a bit of interpretation, but many good scholars read it like this: "A year, two years, and half a year." That would be three-and-a-half years, or, if you accept the ancient Jewish reckoning of three hundred sixty days in a year, a total of . . . exactly 1,260 days again. In Revelation: 1,260 days – or years. And here in Daniel: 1,260 days – or years. A prophetic period of time where this beast, or little horn, would blaspheme God, persecute His people, try to draw worship to himself instead of God, and even try to change God's laws.

Well, what's it mean for us? Simply this: in these last days, stay with God. Worship Him. Worship only Him. Worship Him who created the world, and all of us in it. Beware of any invitation which would draw away your worship. Beware of any spiritual invitation that carries the political taint of "coalition coercion." Beware of any invitation that hints or suggests that God's Law, which never changes, CAN be changed or ignored. If these prophetic words are true, those deceptive invitations have been around for a great many centuries, and are going to be revived or "healed," here in the final generations.

19

SOME LIES ARE WHITE, OTHERS DEADLY

Every now and then it makes for an entertaining, but still painful, hour of television on a drama like *Law and Order*. Someone in a family – usually a child – is desperately ill. Their temperature hovers around 104. An infection is raging out of control. But the parents don't call the doctor. They don't accept an antibiotic pill which could quickly stem the tide. They refuse the option of an operation or a blood transfusion. Instead they just have faith. They pray, while the crisis grows ever more imminent. And before the police can knock down the door and forcibly take the child from the praying parents, the child dies.

Which, of course, leads to the point of drama. Do the prosecutors press charges against the parents? "Reckless endangerment of a minor"? Or do a mother and father have a right to hold to the teachings of their chosen "religion," trusting in faith instead of ambulances and neo-natal units? Even to the point of that slow drive to the cemetery, because it was "God's will"?

Well, the First Amendment intricacies of church and state and spiritual healings are the topic for another time. Suffice it to say at this juncture: Bible truth is something which does make a difference! It does matter what a Christian believes. Would you agree with that? Reading the Bible wrong – or not reading it at all – can be a fatal mistake.

In a *Christianity Today* editorial dating back to May of 1997, Dr. Dean Nelson, professor of journalism at Point Loma Nazarene College in San Diego, wrote about some people who very earnestly followed what they believed. They had what they were sure was The Truth. The title of his piece is "To Heaven on a UFO?" "Heaven's Gate followers believed they could reach paradise by leaving their bodies," he writes, "and joining a UFO that followed the Hale-Bopp comet. They believed that God resided in one of their leaders." And then he adds this chilling P.S. "Much of what they said in their videos and Web sites about community, love, and eternal life I had heard for years in evangelical churches – about death to self and ultimately about death itself."

And we all know where the errors of Marshall Herff Applewhite led his cult followers. Those mistaken ideas – mixed in with some truth – killed those people. They believed a lie and it cost them their lives.

How does this tie in with the warnings in these Three Angels' Messages of Revelation 14? The focus of these seven verses is worship, and the Heaven's Gate cult members worshiped all right. They were more devoted to their religion than most of us are to ours. They made sacrifices for their faith that most of us would never consider.

It's been our careful determination in studying here that the Babylon of the book of Revelation is itself a spiritual power. Remember that it forces the entire world to give IT worship. It's false worship, to be sure. It's coerced worship. It's persecution worship. You can't buy or sell, we read, unless you get the "mark" of this beast in your forehead or in your hand . . . which might mean that you, A) actually believe in this Babylon, in your own mind. Or, B) you simply go along because it IS a coercing, gun-at-your-head, economic-boycott kind of power.

So to all of the other biblical descriptions and clues, if you will, about Babylon, we must add this one more. Yes, it is spiritual. Yes, it is global. Yes, it is coercive. And . . . yes, it involves a *departure* from truth. People will still be sitting in the pews, and they'll still be bowing down. They'll be singing and praying. But, just like the devotees of Heaven's Gate did, they will be embracing falsehood instead of truth.

So right here we have to ask the rhetorical question: Is truth important? Is it life-or-death? Our on-air preachers have proclaimed on *The Voice of Prophecy* many, many times that the Bible tells us Jesus Christ is the only Son of God, AND the only way to salvation. It's the cross's way or no way. Is that vital truth? Is it life-or-death? Absolutely, it is. Moving into the camp of "all roads lead to heaven" would be dangerous indeed. To be wrong on this issue would be a fatal error.

On the other hand, Christian denominations around the world do disagree on many points where, if you found out on the Sea of Glass, you were wrong about it . . . well, it wouldn't matter too much. Speaking of Heaven's Gate, these people decided that celibacy was a requirement of the faith. And we know what lengths they went to in following that doctrine. Other world churches teach it as well: that their priests have to be celibate. Now, I don't find that in the Word of God. I firmly believe that celibacy is an error – and perhaps one the devil has used to tempt and frustrate many people. However, you could be wrong about celibacy and still be saved in the Kingdom of God. St. Augustine once wrote about the many beliefs you or I might be wrong on: "In essentials, unity; in nonessentials, liberty; and in all things, charity."

But what about fatal error . . . the kind where you think some immortal soul inside of you can escape your body after you eat poisoned applesauce and ascend to the next level on a comet? Maybe you remember an Old Testament story where King Saul was worried about an upcoming battle against the Philistines. God didn't seem to be answering him. His prayer life was zero. He was discouraged from chasing his enemy David all over Judea. And he made the terrible decision to go seek out the advice of a witch, a spirit medium. Have you heard of the Witch of Endor?

Now, it's plain fact that God had absolutely forbidden His people to visit witches. Witches were supposed to be executed. Dabbling in the occult, trying to "contact the dead," was a million miles off limits for worshipers of the true God. The possibility for satanic interference, for Satan's evil angels to impersonate a dead person, was just so great. And so God had drawn a huge line in the sand and said, "Don't go there. Don't even THINK of going there. Don't touch that stuff." But Saul went. You can read about it in First Samuel 28.

It's interesting that the NIV Bible scholars seize on this very real possibility of satanic deception here. Was it maybe evil spirits impersonating Samuel? Doesn't the Word of God say in plain English, Ecclesiastes chapter 9, that: "The living know that they shall die, but the dead know not *anything*"? Wouldn't that verse have protected King Saul from being deceived? Wouldn't the truth in that verse have been protection for him? Sure it would. But he ignored the truths God had kindly made plain to him, and went into the dark room where the séance was being held. He listened to the voice of Lucifer. And exactly one day later, having forfeited the protection of God, he was dead.

So I ask again: does it matter what we believe? Is truth important? Is it a big deal if we are in Babylon, worshiping a false organization, and allowing our minds to be fed a mix of truth and error? Very clearly the author of Revelation, John the beloved disciple, believed it was a big deal. Right at the end of the Third Angel's Message, we find that Babylon is going to be destroyed by fire, by the wrath of God. Which means that those who stay IN Babylon, who continue to cling to false worship and false Bible teachings, will be destroyed as well. Is it life and death? Yes it is. No wonder chapter 18 has the mighty warning: "Come OUT of her, My people, before you're caught by her charms. Come out of her before you begin to share in her sins and thus receive her plagues!"

So what does this mean for us? Again, we can make sure we're not worshiping Babylon if we always worship, and only worship, God. But how can we make sure that we don't embrace the deceptions of Babylon here in these final generations of time? How can you know that your friends Lonnie Melashenko and David B. Smith – at least we very smoothly SAY we're your friends, don't we? – aren't giving you 15 minutes of Babylon error right now? Could a radio ministry be a participant in Babylon?

I have a word of protection for you . . . and this isn't a radio word from a human being; it's a divine word from the mouth of Jesus Christ Himself. Is ALL truth important? He said that it was. Does the Bible teach us all truth? He said that too. And rejoice with me over this amazing promise, words of gold for a new millennium, found in John chapter 16. "When He, the Spirit of truth, has come," Jesus says, referring, of course, to the Holy Spirit, "He will guide you into *all* truth." And then this additional promise: "And He will tell you things to come."

I really like how the new paraphrase called *The Message*, by Eugene Peterson, puts it: "But when the Friend comes, the Spirit of the Truth, He will take you *by the hand* and guide you into *all the truth there is*."

Now THAT is protection! Do you want protection from Babylon and its deadly applesauce mix of truth and error? The Holy Spirit IS that protection. He'll tell us what is to come, and He'll guide us into all the truth there is. That's certainly enough to keep us safe.

TWENTY-TWO BIRTHDAY CARDS

Some of us have been getting a "sneak preview" from a brand new Bible correspondence course entitled *Focus on Prophecy*. This exciting project is being masterminded by my VOP associate Kurt Johnson, and has as its focus the book of Revelation. But even before the presses began to roll with these great new lessons [summer 2000], I kind of lifted out a "bootleg" anecdote from one of them. Here it is:

"Laura lost her father to cancer at an early age," he writes, "and missed him keenly in the months after the funeral. He'd been such a loving man. At her next birthday, however, she was astounded to find a letter from Dad addressed to her and bearing the current date. It offered her encouragement and counsel about the challenges she'd face at this stage in her life. On her next birthday, there was another letter from Dad, talking to her about this particular time in her life. And so it went, through every birthday as Laura grew into a mature young woman. Her father, knowing he was dying, had composed a series of letters to her, addressing each special year in her life. It was his way of saying how much he cared about her and her future." And then this summary statement: "That's why God has given us these wonderful prophecies in the Bible. How does it make you feel to know that God loves you so much that He has revealed details about the future?"

That's a great thought question, isn't it? Because this is personal! The 22 chapters in Revelation are like 22 sealed envelopes with my name written on them. Or yours. Considering how vital, and how complex, these mysterious writings by John are, maybe we should space them out, and just read one a year over 22 successive birthdays. But here in these 22 brief chapters, these 404 verses, God is writing us a letter. "Hang in there!" He says. "Dark forces are coming down the highway; they'll try to pull you away from

Me. They're going to persecute. They're going to pervert truth. But if you stay in My care, if you keep focusing on the fact that I'm your Creator and your Protector – if you keep your eyes and your worship focused right here – you're going to be all right."

The late Bible scholar, C. Mervyn Maxwell, and his family grew up in the throes of World War II England. The Blitzkrieg was going on, the blackout nights down in the Tube, the subway, while the bombs were going off overhead. Adolf Hitler was acting like his Panzer divisions and his Luftwaffe were going to sweep across Europe and take it all.

But you know something? Mervyn and his brothers and his mom and dad, all faithful Christians, all prophecy students, sat in their darkened living room and listened to the BBC just like all the others. They heard Winston Churchill's speeches about blood, sweat, and tears. "We will never, never, NEVER give up," and all the rest. And I'm sure they took hope from those words.

But they took even more hope from the words found in their old King James Bibles, the prophetic words from Daniel and Revelation which clearly tell this planet that after four world empires, Babylon, Medo-Persia, Greece, and Rome, there simply would not *ever* be another world tyrant who could dominate all of Europe. Not Charlemagne. Not Napoleon. Not Stalin. And not this latest Gestapo madman. The promises of Daniel and Revelation made it clear that there would not be a "Thousand-Year Reich."

That's not to say that the Maxwell family climbed into hammocks and sipped champagne during the war. We can't point to Bible verses and say, "Not to worry. Jesus is coming; this planet can just go to hell." God expects us to resist evil and stand up against tyranny; that's one of the ways heaven fulfills its promises and prophecies. But when all of human works are said and done, what a comfort it is to know that the Bible puts the power of heaven behind these guarantees.

If these prophecies are new to you, it's kind of raised the temperature in your own spiritual zone. "Judgment is coming!" "Babylon
is fallen!" "The wrath of God poured out." Etc. Etc. There are a
lot of dragons and doom and destruction in these 404 verses, and
we only read about ten of them, total. But please notice with me
here in the chapter of our focus, Revelation 14, that yes, we DO
have this fallen beast. And the smoke of her torment going up forever. That's verse 11. But what's in verse 14? "Then the scene
changed and I saw a white cloud, and someone sitting on it who
looked like Jesus, who was called 'The Son of Man,' with a crown
of solid gold upon His head and a sharp sickle in His hand."

Isn't that tremendous? Wouldn't you like to have that in a birthday
card for you – Jesus on a throne, coming to rescue you? Coming
with a crown for you? What wonderful news that all the doom and
the demons is followed by a Deliverer.

Revelation chapter 16 has as a subtitle: "The Vials of Wrath." It's
fearsome stuff: the seven last plagues. Which, for those who rebel
against God, are going to be a nightmare beyond comprehension.
Notice: for those who rebel against God. But God lovingly calls
us to NOT rebel, to instead worship Him as Creator. Do we have
to experience the seven last plagues of chapter 16? No!

And what comes later? In Revelation chapter 20, Satan is bound
and rendered helpless. That's good news, isn't it? I don't want to
skip that. Just a few verses later, after one last gasp from our
ancient enemy, Lucifer and his minions are finally destroyed forever in the lake of fire. Tragically, those who tenaciously cling to his
falsehoods, who reject God as Creator and Jesus Christ as
Redeemer, share their fate. Is that bad news for us? It doesn't
have to be . . . because all through Revelation we're invited, in
those 22 birthday cards, to embrace God as Creator. To accept
Jesus as Savior. That's pure protection from the horrors of

Revelation chapter 20 . . . which is followed by the incredible good news of chapter 21: "The New Heaven and the New Earth." "And I John saw the holy city, new Jerusalem, coming down from God out of heaven, prepared as a bride adorned for her husband. . . . And God Himself shall be with them, and be their God. And God shall wipe away all tears from their eyes; and there shall be no more death, neither sorrow, nor crying, neither shall there be any more pain: for the former things are passed away."

Let me make a full and free confession: there are things in Revelation I don't understand. But these verses right here – I DO understand. No more death. I understand that. No more pain; I don't find much mystery or apocalyptic confusion in those three words. No sorrow. No crying. Are you in any doubt about what those verses promise for you and me? God living with us, dwelling with us? WITH US?! I'm not baffled a whole lot by that. And I've got to tell you: I want it. I want it bad.

As we close, I think the best thing might be to quietly return to the very end of the message of this third Angel. The warnings have been given. The safeguards have been detailed. And then John the Revelator, who himself had endured a personal microcosm of some of these persecutions – false worship, dangerous doctrines, plagues and apostasies all around – gives us these sure words: "These things that I saw," he writes, "will call for special endurance on the part of God's people who keep the commandments of God . . . AND are faithful to Jesus."

And I'd like to end with those three words right there: "Faithful to Jesus." At this very moment in time – and for all time – I want to be "faithful to Jesus." My safeguard today isn't in figuring out these prophecies. My salvation doesn't come from deciphering what "666" represents. My heavenly home isn't going to be given to me because I drew a timeline and guessed right about what the Mark of the Beast is. No, I'm looking forward to living in the City of God because I've been blessed to have a relationship of being faithful to Jesus.

There might be many differences today between "me and thee" as
we turn this final page. I'm Protestant; maybe you're Catholic.
I'm a writer and lay preacher; maybe you're a lay *person*. Maybe
you're in prison as you read these words. But if in these end
times, *you* are faithful to Jesus, and *I* am faithful to Jesus, then
we're going to be together in that great multitude described in
Revelation 19.

"Even so, come, Lord Jesus."